150 Years of the District

Photo Credits

London Transport Museum 5, 8, 9, 10, 14 top, 15 top, 16, 17, 18, 20, 23, 25, 26, 27, 29 top, 30, 32-42, 43 top, 44, 47, 48, 51 top, 52, 53, 55, 57 top, 59 top, 60 bottom, 62, 63 top, 64, 65, 66, 68, 70 bottom
Roy Allen collection 57 bottom
Capital Transport colour views on 14, 15, 28, 50, 51, 70 top and centre, 73 bottom, 80 bottom
Capital Transport collection 13, 19, 21 top, 28 top, 32, 43 bottom, 50 top, 60 top, 61 top, 61 bottom, 63 bottom
Colour-Rail 45 top, 59 bottom
Jim Connor collection 58
The Engineer 12 top
Getty Images 6/7, 24
John Gillham 21 bottom
Brian Hardy 45 bottom
Mike Horne 73 top
Mike Horne collection 54
Paul Moss collection 69
Kim Rennie 67, 71 top, 74-79, 80 top

ISBN 978 1 85414 435 5

Published by
Capital Transport Publishing Ltd
www.capitaltransport.com

Printed by Parksons Graphics

150 Years of the District

Capital Transport

Building and Financing the District Railway
Antony Badsey-Ellis

The origins of the Metropolitan District Railway (today's District Line) lie in the success of the Metropolitan Railway following its opening in 1863, and the difficulties in raising sufficient capital to extend the Met at both ends to form a loop along the north side of the River Thames. It was the latter which caused the promoters to establish the District as a separate company, with its own powers to raise capital but with four directors and its engineer, John Fowler, in common with the Met. The new company's first Act of Parliament (in 1864) gave it powers to raise £3·6 million through the sale of shares, and another £1·2 million from loans.

The authorised line was to connect with the Met at South Kensington and Trinity Square, Tower Hill; the Met had two Acts approved in the same year giving it the power to extend its line to the same points from its existing termini at Paddington and Moorgate respectively. Together the railways described in the three Acts would form a continuous circuit with the pioneer line forming much of the northern side, the District the southern side, and the new Met extensions the western and eastern sides.

West of South Kensington, the District was to continue on to form junctions with the West London Extension Railway; one, facing north, just south of Addison Road station, and the other, facing north, at West Brompton station. Today these form the Olympia and northern section of the Wimbledon branches.

Construction of the District began in the west, leaving the more expensive section in the City until later. A consortium of contractors helped promote the line from the outset, and, as was typical for the day, also provided financial support. All were experienced in railway construction, and it was thought that their involvement would provide added confidence to investors. Sadly, this was not the case and one of the contractors, Peto & Betts, became insolvent in 1866 when the bank of Overend, Gurney & Company collapsed.

The railway was constructed as a series of covered ways, but where possible, open sections of cutting were made. The original Metropolitan Railway had built long sections of continuous covered way, which rapidly filled with smoke and steam as the trains passed through. Regular openings would help keep the air in the tunnels tolerable for the staff and passengers.

Work started on building the District in February 1865. The Gloucester Road marked the western edge of built-up London, and so to the west of here the line was made in an open cutting. Eastwards, it cut across the existing street pattern as far as St James's Park. It then ran beneath roads to the new Victoria Embankment, which it was to follow as far as Blackfriars, before heading away from the river beneath the new Queen Victoria Street, up as far as Cannon Street and then on to Trinity Square.

The many houses beneath which the line passed had to be underpinned or else demolished; some of those that were demolished were rebuilt, but there is still a line of gardens and green spaces that follows along the line of the route, such as Cadogan Gardens just west of Sloane Square. The occasional opening between adjacent covered ways remains too, providing glimpses of daylight to passengers.

The work of building the railway was largely manual, although assisted by limited machinery such as steam shovels, an early type of excavator. Sewers and other services beneath the streets had to be reconstructed to pass along the edges of the streets, behind the walls forming the new covered way. Once this work was complete a pair of parallel trenches was cut in which the side walls for the covered way were made, 25ft apart. The steam shovels were used for this work, running on temporary tracks laid along the line of the workings. With the side walls completed, the roof section could be built. In many cases this was an elliptical arch formed of five rings of brickwork giving a clearance at the centre

of 15ft 9 above rail level. Where the line could not be made deep enough for this type of roof, the side walls were spanned by large metal girders placed 8ft apart. Brickwork arches were formed between adjacent girders, and these were then covered with a layer of asphalt on which the road surface was then laid.

The earth and soil forming the core of the covered way was only excavated once the roofing work was under way. This avoided the need to excavate a large amount of material at one time, for which there was only very limited storage space. This material was removed along the line of the railway in carts on temporary rails to points where it could be conveniently brought to the surface for carting away. The base of the covered way - the invert - was constructed of either brick or concrete, together with a drainage channel. The permanent way, comprising the ballast and the rails, was then laid on top.

The line in the Westminster area cut through much sand and gravel, and this was reused to make the massive quantities of concrete and mortar required. Any excess was sold to other contractors for use elsewhere in London. The ground here was very wet, and pumps were installed to remove an estimated 4,000 gallons of water per minute from the workings. An unusual feature of the tunnel as it passed Westminster Abbey was the insertion of a layer of peat, 7ft thick, behind the walls, to reduce the vibrations from the railway being transmitted to the Abbey.

Above: Work to construct the MDR near to South Kensington in around 1868. The rings of brickwork forming the tunnel crowns can be seen. There are two tunnels under construction, one for the MDR and the other for the parallel Metropolitan Railway tracks.

Overleaf: Construction of the cut-and-cover tunnels at Bedford Gardens, south of Notting Hill Gate station, in 1867. On the left of the picture is the wall of a house, showing where its neighbouring property has been demolished. The gap remains today.

By mid-1866, it was estimated that around 2,000 men, 200 horses, and 58 'engines' were involved in the construction. The vast number of bricks required to form the sides of the cuttings, the covered ways, and the various buildings were made in two kilns located at Earl's Court, then a small village just west of the built-up edge of London. Some 140 million were required for the line, and they were baked from London clay removed from the workings.

Effort was focused on the section between South Kensington and Westminster initially, enabling this section of the line to open on Christmas Eve 1868. By this point, around £3 million had been spent – the whole of the capital that it had thus far been able to raise. The public was losing interest in buying railway shares as the returns were proving to be rather less than promised. However, by having a line to South Kensington, through trains could operate round onto the Met, which would not have been possible had the District built an isolated section of line serving the City. That said, two short sections of tunnel were built for the District in front of both Blackfriars and Cannon Street main-line stations during this period.

Towards the City

One particular problem that occurred as a result of the delays in raising the finance was in the section of line east of Westminster. Here the railway was to follow the line of the new Victoria Embankment, being placed within the embankment structure. The ideal situation would have been to construct the two together, but the delays in raising finance caused the District to slip behind schedule. Since the Embankment was a key piece of infrastructure for London, including as it did the new Northern Low Level Sewer, it could not be delayed. There were also disputes with the Metropolitan Board of Works, who were building the embankment, over responsibility for compensation payments to the owners of the riverside wharves eliminated by the new structure.

Below: A cross-section of Charing Cross (now Embankment) station, published as part of a poster in 1914 to advertise the extension of the Hampstead Tube, seen bottom right.

Opposite: An excerpt from the first edition of The District Railway Map of London (dated 1873), showing the Inner Circle incomplete between Mansion House and Moorgate Street. Both the MDR and the MR lines are bold, with other railway companies in thinner red lines. Note also the old spelling of 'Edgeware Road'.

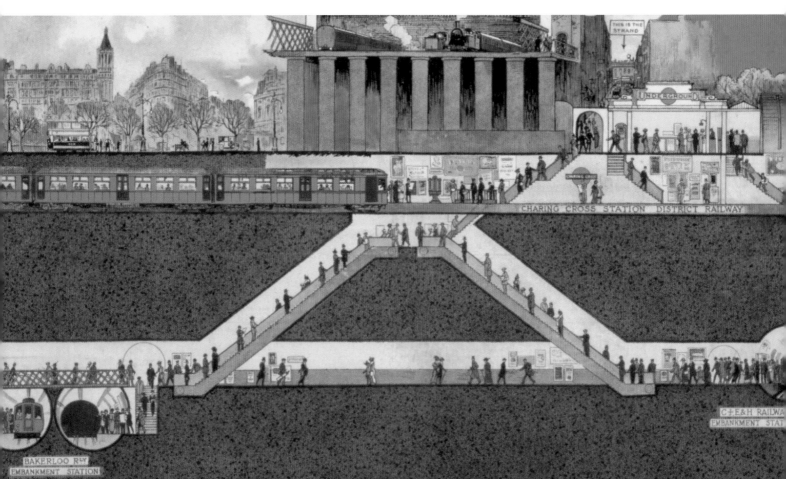

In order to allow the District to continue, an Act of 1869 permitted it to sell £1·5 million of preference shares in place of the remaining unsold ordinary shares from the original issue. These shares would pay interest at 5%, and were therefore more attractive to investors. Money was also now coming in from the tickets sold on the first section of the route. With the money raised, the line continued to Blackfriars via stations at Charing Cross (now called Embankment) and Temple. The delay meant that there was additional work in digging out some of the soil used to construct the Victoria Embankment.

Blackfriars gave particular problems to the contractors, since the covered way had to be threaded below several existing tunnels and above the tunnel holding the old Fleet River, which was effectively a major sewer discharging into the Thames. The work involved reconstructing the Fleet's tunnel to be wider and flatter, so that the maximum flow would remain the same but the railway could have an acceptable headroom. This section of the District opened to the public on 30 May 1870.

The following year the District extended one station eastwards, to Mansion House. The tunnel followed the line of Queen Victoria Street, with the new terminus located on the south side of Cannon Street. On the same date, 3 July, new platforms constructed by the District

at High Street Kensington were opened. A week later, it opened its own platforms at South Kensington, parallel to those of the Met and on the southern side. This gave it a fully independent route round to High Street Kensington, without having to impinge on the tracks of the Metropolitan. The District also began operating its own trains; previously it had paid the MR to provide the trains over its railway, but simmering disagreements between the two had led to it ordering its own locomotives and carriages. From this day, both companies operated their own trains over the full length of the line between Mansion House and Moorgate Street, advertised as the 'Inner Circle' (despite the obvious gap then remaining through the City).

Unlike the temporary termini of Westminster and Blackfriars, Mansion House was built with four tracks and three double-sided platforms between them, as well as a single platform serving the south side of the southernmost track. There were also facilities to load coal and water onto locomotives. It appeared that the District expected this to remain the terminus for some time. Despite the section of tunnel just to the east, at Cannon Street, which still remained unused, any further extension eastwards was going to be expensive. Land in the City was at a premium, and the existing buildings were expensive and heavy, making any underpinning works complex.

Westward extensions

The Government and the public became increasingly frustrated during the 1870s at the lack of progress in completing the connection between Mansion House and Moorgate Street. The Met was in a better financial position than the District and opened short extensions eastwards, first to Liverpool Street, and then to Aldgate. The District, for its part, saw a greater opportunity for profit by extending west to the then separate town of Hammersmith. Its fragile finances meant that the extension was promoted as a separate company, which was to build the line but then allow the District to run the trains and collect the revenue in exchange for money to pay its shareholders a dividend. The extension, which opened on 9 September 1874, ran through open countryside on the level, except at the terminus where it was placed into a wide cutting between brick retaining walls.

A short distance to the west, the London & South Western Railway (LSWR) owned a line leading to Richmond, which was constructed on a series of viaducts and embankments. The MDR saw an opportunity for an ever greater extension with minimal building work, and in 1875 gained authority to connect with, and run its trains over, the LSWR tracks. Hammersmith station was reconstructed with more platforms, and a complex piece of tunnelling took the tracks beneath the roadway before emerging to the south of the LSWR viaduct and rising rapidly to the level of the viaduct tracks. Work progressed quickly, and the extension opened on 1 June 1877.

With this link opened, the District lost no time in promoting another extension from the LSWR tracks in Chiswick to Acton and Ealing, terminating next to the Great Western Railway's station at Ealing and opening on 1 July 1879. This is today's Ealing Broadway station.

Ealing Broadway station, showing the plethora of signs and advertisements that accumulated across stations in the Victorian era. This building was replaced in 1911 by a more imposing structure in Portland stone.

Later in the 1870s, the District decided to extend the short West Brompton branch which, despite the original intentions, had not connected with the West London Extension Railway (WLER) but instead terminated in platforms alongside. The extension took the branch into a tunnel beneath the WLER, and then onto a viaduct snaking above the streets of Fulham to a station at Putney Bridge, overlooking the Thames. Opened on 1 March 1880, it was further extended nine years later when the LSWR constructed a branch on the south side of the River Thames from its main line at Wimbledon, and linked the two with a large bridge.

One further westward connection opened on 1 May 1883. This was another surface line linking Mill Hill Park (now Acton Town) with Hounslow, and like the Hammersmith extension was promoted as a separate company, the Hounslow & Metropolitan Railway. It was built easily, passing through open countryside.

Completing the Circle

Back with the inner circle route, the companies resisted the pressure from the public, press and government to complete the line. Instead an independent Inner Circle Completion Company received Parliamentary approval to construct the missing link in 1874, but found it impossible to raise the finance. It was not until the late 1870s that the Met and the District began to work together to promote a joint Act in 1879 for the remaining part of the circle.

Some money was contributed from the local authorities, who hoped to reduce street congestion, and work started in autumn 1882. The tunnel beneath Cannon Street was built deeper than the previous sections, so that it avoided interfering with the existing cellars. Shafts were sunk from the road level, and the tunnel was carefully excavated, beams being inserted

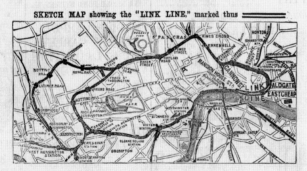

The Metropolitan Inner Circle Completion Railway was promoted independently, following frustration with the slow progress of the District and Metropolitan. This is from its newspaper advertisement attempting (unsuccessfully) to raise the money to build the line through the City.

below the buildings' foundations to provide support until the permanent concrete and brick walls were strong enough to provide this function. This section was built with an elliptical arched roof.

New stations were opened at Cannon Street, Monument, and Mark Lane, the latter replacing a temporary wooden station built by the MR a short distance away after they had rapidly extended their line from Aldgate in September 1882. Beyond Mark Lane, the new line continued to a junction with the Met and then via stations at Aldgate East and St Mary's to a connection with the East London Railway (ELR) just south of that company's Whitechapel station. The Met also built a connection between Liverpool Street and Aldgate East, thus forming a large triangular junction on the eastern edge of the City of London. The District built a short spur from St Mary's to a terminal station at Whitechapel, affording interchange with the ELR as well as providing its passengers with direct access to the busy Whitechapel district of the East End.

Above: Work to construct the tunnel near Cannon Street, showing the primitive conditions, including naked gas flames to illuminate the site. The buildings along the street were expensively underpinned in order to accommodate the railway tunnel and replacement sewers beneath.

A through District train of the first design of steam stock, on a journey from Richmond to the LBSC station at New Cross, approaches Gunnersbury. The connection to the East London Railway was made at St Mary's Curve.

Out to the east

Another 'independent' railway company, the Whitechapel & Bow Railway, was promoted to extend the District 2¼ miles east from Whitechapel to a junction with the main line London, Tilbury & Southend Railway (LTSR). The W&BR was supported by both the District and the LTSR as it would give the latter company a route into the City for its trains, beyond its congested Fenchurch Street terminus. It was authorised by Parliament in August 1897. Although promoted separately from the two companies, both subscribed to its shares and agreed to jointly construct and operate it.

The W&BR led from the open-air platforms at Whitechapel, immediately over the East London Railway, and into a new covered way beneath the Mile End Road. Like the completion of the Inner Circle, it was excavated from a number of shafts sunk from the street, thus avoiding the enormous disruption of the early cut-and-cover construction. This was especially important as a double line of tram tracks ran down the centre of the road, and these were supported on timber decking as the underground work proceeded. Where it crossed the Regent's Canal, between new stations at Stepney Green and Mile End, two cast-iron tubes each 18ft in diameter were constructed, being very similar to the tube tunnels being built deep under central London. Hand mining was used for this 50 yard length of the railway, without the need for tunnelling shields.

The easternmost station on the W&BR was at Bow Road, beyond which the line curved to the south-east, entered a cutting, and rose steeply to join the LTSR at Campbell Road Junction. Train services began over this route on 2 June 1902.

Holders of debenture stock in the MDR received interest on their investments on a half-yearly basis. Statements such as this were sent to inform them how much interest they had earned.

The Upper half of this Sheet is to be detached from the Warrant, and retained for the Information of the Proprietor.

METROPOLITAN DISTRICT RAILWAY COMPANY.

No. 235

Proprietor, *Sir John R H Maxwell ror*

INTEREST ON DEBENTURE STOCK for the Half-year ending 31st December, 1899.

Payable on and after 1st January, 1900.

STATEMENT OF INTEREST.

		Amount of Interest.		
		£	s.	d.
On	Debenture Stock, @ 6 per cent. per annum	15	5	7
On *764*	do. @ 4 „ „			
	Less Income Tax @ 8d. in the £	.	10	2
		£ 14	15	5

I hereby certify that I have deducted from this Interest the amount of Income Tax stated above, and I further certify that the amount of the tax so deducted will be paid by me to the proper officer for the receipt of taxes.

St. James' Park Station, London, S.W., *30th December*, 1899.   WM. JONES, *Secretary.*

The Inland Revenue Department will receive this statement as a voucher in claiming repayment of Income Tax, where the Proprietor is entitled to claim exemption or abatement, and where such is required, this portion of the sheet must be preserved for the purpose.

N.B.—Any change of Address should be specially notified to the Secretary by separate Letter, for record in the Company's Books.

Then and Now: GLOUCESTER ROAD IN 1868 AND TODAY

Then and Now: EARL'S COURT IN 1878 AND TODAY

Working on the District 1
Mike Horne

When the District opened in 1868 the operation of the new railway was contracted out to the Metropolitan Railway which provided the train service and all the staff and maintained the infrastructure. It was not until 3 June 1871 that the District ran the railway itself, at which point it needed its first manpower. Some staff were allowed to transfer from the Metropolitan but many new people were also brought in, some (but not all) from other railways. The District functioned in much the same way as any other railway at that time, the fact of it being a so-called 'underground' railway not requiring any different arrangement.

Stations were at first run by inspectors (station masters came later) with other grades including booking clerks, ticket collectors and porters. The porters were the most versatile grade and announced trains, helped passengers on and off and made sure that all the doors were firmly closed and locked before the train started. They were also available to help carry passenger's luggage, but no further than to or from the station entrance.

Booking clerks were never part of the uniformed staff and were regarded as clerical staff, responsible for issuing passengers with tickets and the intricate process of accounting for the cash taken and reconciling this with the value of the tickets sold. In those days, each possible journey from every station had its own specific ticket and included variants for each class, including return tickets, as well as a host of special tickets for particular types of traveller. Booking clerks had to work quickly and accurately whilst answering a barrage of questions about train times, changes along the journey, departure platform and so on. The counterpart was the ticket collector who had to check tickets on entry to a platform (and collect them on exit) and recognise at a glance whether whatever was being shown was correct or not. There were also travelling inspectors who checked tickets on route or on trains and who sought to detect fraudulent travel. The signalling was all manually controlled by signal-boxes located at each station, the signalmen also coming under the control of the station inspector.

A group of station staff and locomotive men at Mill Hill Park (now Acton Town) station at an unknown date between 1884 and 1903. The locomotive stands outside a small shed east of the station and the two men on the left are probably its driver and fireman. Just visible on right are two permanent way men at work.

Early photos of the District are rare but this one is taken in May 1876 at the original station at Earl's Court. On the locomotive, the driver is perched at the left and the fireman is on the right, with his hand on the hand-brake. The signalman looks on, from his box at the east end of the platform. The identities of the rest of the group are less clear, but the uniformed staff seem to be wearing porter's uniforms. The superior civilian gentleman with beard and hat, from his demeanour, is probably from the locomotive department and perhaps an inspector.

The uniformed staff also included train staff, who comprised the guard (who was in charge and rode at the rear) and brakesmen (later called under-guards) who travelled at the front and were sometimes called front guards. Apart from determining when it was safe for a train to proceed, they also helped the driver bring the train to rest using handbrakes. After air brakes were installed, drivers could usually apply all the braking necessary. Trains were hauled by steam locomotives operated by a driver and fireman who were part of the locomotive department (responsible to the company's engineer). As on other railways, the usual line of progression was from engine cleaner to fireman and then driver. Enginemen were competent practical engineers who were expected to get their locomotives out of trouble when defects arose. However, we know that during periods of expansion, the District recruited from other railways and the transferred staff were allowed to keep their grade.

Other staff were required to maintain the track, stations, tunnels and rolling stock and most of this work was concentrated at the main workshops at Lillie Bridge where the company's engineer had his office. Call staff were located around the system to deal quickly with failures likely to affect the service. Signal repairmen, for example, were located at Victoria and carriage examiners at Mansion House.

Pay and conditions varied only slightly during the steam era. In the 1890s we find a driver explaining he was paid eight shillings a day, which he thought was 'good' pay and put him on the same footing as a policeman and other 'respectable people'. Drivers then got one day off a fortnight and this pay equates to around £130 a year. It would be fair to say this represented more than double the average working class wage at that time and by some measures appears of the same order as train operators today.

Typical hours might comprise a ten hour shift with meals taken as opportunity arose, often on the footplate. Duties varied daily and continuous running around the Circle Line (then operated in part by District staff) was unpopular and usually restricted to one day a week.

The porter's day consisted of either an early or late shift, both of ten hours, and these were occupied by a myriad of odd jobs such as station cleaning and maintaining the station oil lamps as well as more mundane duties such as safely seeing the trains away and assisting passengers with their luggage. For this, he might get a pound a week or 22 shillings if it included a Sunday. This produced nearly £55 a year (an average worker's wage) but he might make a little more from tips.

For many years the lower grades of staff did not receive a pension, resulting in some staff (including drivers) continuing to work into their seventies (retirement at 65 was required only in 1923). This practice was common amongst railway companies and a number of provident associations were founded by the men that could for modest weekly contributions fund a small pension on retirement and sick pay if they became ill. Several of these were supported by the companies and District staff were often members of at least one of these bodies. One was the Metropolitan District Railway Mutual Provident Society, formed in 1887 and based at Lillie

Below: This impression of a porter dates from c1885 and perhaps accurately represents the slightly dishevelled appearance of the lowest grade of staff who was expected to hump and carry passengers' luggage and parcels from surface to platform or back upon request, attend to the opening and closing of carriage doors, bawl out the name of the station and the destination of trains as they passed through and have an encyclopaedic knowledge of the system to answer passengers' queries. Their troubles were leavened by the tips a keen and friendly service might produce ('soliciting' tips was prohibited but, after all, declining them if offered might cause offence).

Below right: A District Railway guard towards the end of the steam era. The guard was part of the passenger department and was in charge of the train and responsible for the safety and well being of the passengers (the enginemen were part of the engineering department). The guard was expected to appear smart and efficient. The brass buttons bear the letters DR too.

"MY FRIENDLY PORTER."

Lots Road Power House in the early 1930s, one of the electrical staff attending to one of the generators that supplied the District and much of the tube network. Until London Transport was formed, the power house was run by a joint committee of the District and the London Electric Railway but employed its own electrical staff.

Bridge. For office staff there was the Railway Officials Association, formed in 1873 and based at Mansion House station. It was not until 1899 that office staff were given a superannuation fund enabling the provision of a pension, though it was only some years later that operating staff got a company pension. The District also supported the provision of a savings bank for the staff, which allowed them to save regularly and securely.

Electrification meant a profound change to the way train and maintenance staff were organised although it had less impact on station staff. The need was for men to be selected for training as electric drivers (graded 'motorman') and other staff to be trained to act as 'conductors' (as the man in charge was now to be called) with other train staff to assist with the doors and in getting trains away at stations. It was proposed to make sure at least one other member of the train staff should be able to drive the train in an emergency. This meant bringing all train staff into one department and by a process of selection offering the new motorman's jobs first to existing suitable locomotive drivers and, topping up, if necessary, from the firemen. Conductors were selected from the head and, if necessary, under-guards. Staff found unsuitable or surplus for these jobs would be offered jobs as gatemen, to operate the doors under the control of the conductor. It was hoped to absorb most of the existing staff this way.

The drivers were required to be medically examined and pass a test to prove they were suitable even for training (which hurdles do not seem to have applied to locomotivemen). The new American managers did not believe the electric trains required the skills of a steam man and wanted to pay the men less, claiming they should be on a par with tramwaymen. As railway staff were not then represented by trades unions there was nobody to put forward much of a defence to this and pay was significantly reduced, though there was some protection for existing staff. Motormen were to receive between 35 shillings and 42 shillings and sixpence a week depending on length of service in that grade or as a steam driver. Gatemen got slightly more than half the motorman's rate with conductors in between.

The District was permanently impoverished and it is a surprise that the four staff who had been required on each steam-hauled train were to be increased to seven on an electric train – a driver, conductor and five gatemen, one who acted as front conductor. This number of gatemen was necessary to operate the pneumatically controlled doors but these were found not to work very well and were soon made hand-operated, at a practical level being opened by the passengers and closed by staff. It was quickly decided to remove some of the gatemen and get platform staff to close certain of the doors, but by the end of the First World War most trains were being operated by only the two conductors. When 'starting devices' (a means by which the rear conductor could tell the driver it was safe to start) were installed in the mid-1920s, then all but 8-car trains were reduced to a driver and guard (as the conductor had become called). Two guards were still needed on very long trains to lock doors that would stop beyond platform limits, but from 1933 the front man was withdrawn and extra platform staff maintained vigilance instead.

With the thinning out of train staff it became impossible to ensure every door was in fact closed before a train started, or to stop passengers opening doors in hot weather. This situation was only quite slowly felt unacceptable and it was not until the late 1930s that a satisfactory form of air-worked door system began to be introduced, and well into the 1950s that the District was fully converted to air-door operation under the overriding control of one guard (who remained the emergency train driver).

When the District came under the control of the (at first) American-owned Underground Group there was little attempt to interfere with existing pay and conditions beyond those necessary for electrification. The growth in importance of trades unions and the massive distortions in pay and cost of living arising from the First World War needed pay and conditions across the whole of the Underground network to be addressed. A determined effort was made to associate particular rates of pay for particular types of work and the pay and conditions of District staff were substantially harmonised with all of the group's railways. By 1928 drivers were receiving between 72 shillings and 90 shillings a week depending on time in the grade, guards received between 50 shillings and 65 shillings and porters 46 shillings. To give some context it appears guards were paid a little more than the average wage, porters rather less and drivers considerably more. The lowest of the seven grades of stationmaster received about the same as a driver but the highest grade got nearly double that. All the various grades of booking clerk were paid more than drivers though.

It was not until after the First World War that conditions across the railway industry became more uniform and the aspiration of the 8-hour day was introduced (in turn making a 3-shift system necessary, a system still in use). Gradually the idea of a day off a week became the norm, with Sundays regarded as overtime, though always part of the roster.

Below left: A District guard in standard Underground Railway uniform in January 1924. He is using his flag to pull a wire that operated a bell near the driver to indicate the train was ready to depart. Another of the guard's duties was to display the correct destination and non stop boards along the train, one set of which is just visible at left.

Below: A District Line guard illustrating the standard Underground Railways uniform used across the network.

Above: The District's works at Ealing Common, probably around 1910, showing work taking place of sets of bogies. As with several other District images, most of the staff seem keen to be included in the photograph.

Below: A train of hand-worked door stock towards the end of its life in the early 1950s. When new, staff would have closed these at stations but by the time of this photo it was not unusual for doors to be left open by passengers during travel in warmer weather.

The American Influence
Dr Piers Connor

In the 1880s, the District ran steam train services over much of the same system as we see today, i.e. to Ealing, Richmond and Wimbledon in the west but only as far as Whitechapel in the east. In a hate-hate relationship with the Metropolitan Railway, a relationship which, some would say, isn't entirely dead even today, the two railways jointly operated the Circle Line. In terms of finance, the Metropolitan was relatively prosperous but the District was in a dreadful state and things weren't about to get better.

The American influence on the District began as early as 1875, when the District purchased the air brake system designed by George Westinghouse, but this was only a single early indicator of the future pattern of US influence. Then, in 1881 an American engineer came to attend an electrical exhibition at the Crystal Palace. His name was Frank Julian Sprague and he was to have a profound influence on the development of electric traction around the world and in particular on the District Railway. During his visit Sprague travelled regularly on the steam-operated lines of the District and Metropolitan and he became convinced that here was a system which needed conversion to electric power. He wanted to rid the tunnels of steam and smoke and he had a dream that electric trains would one day do the job. He told the story later that he seriously considered staying on in London just so he could achieve that dream. He didn't stay then – electric traction technology had not developed sufficiently to allow its use on railways – but his dream did come true when the multiple unit electric traction system that he invented replaced steam in London some 24 years later.

A few years later in 1890, the electrically operated City & South London Railway opened to the public. Over the next ten years, two new electric underground lines opened, the Waterloo & City Railway and the Central London Railway (in 1898 and 1900 respectively), using direct current (DC) equipment and this encouraged other tube railway schemes across central London, three of which were to become the Bakerloo, Hampstead (now Northern) and Piccadilly lines.

The new and planned electric tube lines all cut into the central area ringed by the Circle Line. With the Circle being steam operated, passengers had long complained about the smoke-filled tunnels, the soot-covered trains and stations and the discomforts of the heat and fumes they endured when travelling underground. People avoided the tunnels as much as possible, especially in hot weather. In 1898, an inquiry by the Board of Trade into air quality in the Circle's tunnels rather obviously suggested that the best solution was electrification. Indeed, since the new tube lines offered the possibility of a vastly superior journey once they were opened, they were going to create a huge dent in the District's (and Metropolitan's) income. The District, especially, couldn't take much of that and survive.

In the late 1890s, electric traction was still a relatively new idea. There were a number of tramways and urban routes in the US which had introduced electric trains, many of them using electric motors and controllers devised by Sprague. In Britain, the Liverpool Overhead Railway, as well as the two new tube lines in London, opened with electric traction. When the Central London Railway opened in 1900 between Shepherds Bush and the Bank it was in direct competition with the District's route to Mansion House, which is a short walk from the Bank. The District, being in a bad way financially, had little chance of raising capital for improvements. Even so, the District's management was forced to get into negotiations with the Metropolitan Railway over how things might be improved. Electrification was obviously the only way forward and, with their joint operation of the Circle, they had to choose the same system. So they agreed, in May 1898, to try out an experimental installation of electric traction between High Street Kensington and Earl's Court.

Electrical Train and Tracks at Earl's Court Station.

During the summer of 1900, the District Railway and the Metropolitan Railway conducted a joint experiment into electric traction using a specially built 6-car train (seen here at Earl's Court) which shuttled between Earl's Court and High Street Kensington.

The Experimental Train

The Earl's Court experiment used a special 6-coach train, ordered in May 1899 from Brown Marshall & Co. of Saltley, Birmingham (later absorbed into the group that eventually became Metro Cammell) which was delivered in late 1899 to the District's depot at Lillie Bridge. The electrical equipment was supplied by Siemens. Trial running started early in December 1899 and continued spasmodically up to 21 May 1900, when public operation began. The trial ended in November 1900.

The experimental train was still running when, on 3 August 1900, nine different firms were invited to tender for the electrification of the Circle. Two suppliers for the electrification project became what we would call today "preferred bidders" – British Thomson-Houston (BTH), the UK arm of the US General Electric Company, and Ganz & Co. of Hungary. BTH proposed the DC 3rd rail system, already in place on the Central London and City & South London railways, while Ganz offered a 3000-volt, 3 phase AC system requiring three conductors – twin overhead wires for two phases and the running rails for the third phase. The electrification committee came down in favour of Ganz, without a doubt because it was the cheapest offer but almost certainly against the advice of any pragmatic electrical engineer of the time.

Charles Tyson Yerkes, the American financier who arranged the finance and technical expertise for the electrification of the District Railway. The influence of Yerkes and his team survives on the Underground to this day.

The Americans Arrive

In the event, the whole question of the choice of electrical system was turned on its head by the inability of the District Railway to raise capital in London. They turned to the US for it, where a certain Charles Tyson Yerkes was persuaded to lead a financial consortium to pay for both the District's electrification and the building of several tube lines. Yerkes brought his technical advisor to London, one James Russell Chapman, who had considerable experience of setting up electric railways in the US, notably in Chicago. Chapman quickly realised the weaknesses of the Ganz system and set his mind in favour of DC traction, similar to the BTH proposal, already used in the US and by the other underground railways in London. This was in direct opposition to the joint electrification committee's choice of Ganz and it set in motion months of argument between the District and Metropolitan, which ended up going to arbitration. The arbitrator's decision, which was in favour of the District's DC system, was made in December 1901. As is often the way in such things, it is probable that the Metropolitan only fought the District over the DC proposal because Ganz were paying their costs.

From this point on, the Americanisation of the District was total. American money meant American men. In addition to Chapman, Yerkes brought with him F. D. Ward, the master mechanic and rolling stock engineer, who was to give his name to the coupler used for the electric trains on the Underground for the next 30 years, Zac E. Knapp, the electrical engineer who later took over from Chapman as chief engineer, S.B. Fortenbaugh (seconded from General Electric) and five other American engineers who supervised the installation of lifts, electrical systems and telephones, traction power and permanent way. All of them eventually went home apart from Knapp who stayed and became a British citizen. It was said to be Fortenbaugh who persuaded Chapman to adopt the 4-rail traction system as the best solution for the District electrification.

Another American who was to have a huge influence on the District and, later on, the Underground, was William Sebastian Graff-Baker. He joined the District as an apprentice at Ealing Common depot in 1909 and later rose through the ranks to become Chief Mechanical Engineer of the Underground in 1936. He was responsible for importing some of the American ideas used in London from the 1930s for new traction control systems, door systems, automatic couplers and electro-pneumatic brake systems on trains.

American Design

In 1903, the District acquired two experimental 7-car trains for their South Harrow line. They were used to test all the new traction and signalling systems intended for the District and tube lines. In looks, the cars were pure 'wild west', with clerestory roofs, gated, open end platforms and straight, match-boarded sides, enhanced by curve-topped windows. The design was based on cars used in New York, Boston and Chicago.

The car roof was the two-level arrangement we call "clerestory" but it was originally written "clear storey" in a pure description of what it was – the central, upper level of the roof separated from the lower level and supported by glazed panels. Some of the panels could be opened to provide ventilation in the warmer weather. The ends of the roof sloped down to the front and rear of the car in typical American fashion and the driving ends were decorated with lamps on the roof end. In another Americanism, the electric lamps on the car ends were called 'marker lights', an expression which survived on the Underground until very recently.

The fleet of 60 x 7-car trains bought for the District's main line electrification in 1905 (later known as the B Stock), was broadly similar to the experimental cars but the ends were enclosed and doors were pneumatically operated. The door system was crude and unreliable and was withdrawn after only three years in operation. Air door systems didn't return to the District until the late 1930s but even these were based on an American system introduced into London on the tube lines in the early 1920s.

The traction control system used on the B Stock and the other tube lines was based on Sprague's inventions, tried first on a Chicago Elevated line in 1897 and subsequently taken over by General Electric and sold here by BTH. Sprague's vision of an electric Circle had arrived.

The cast steel bogies supplied for the District's fleet were also American, being designed by Frank Hedley, who was one of Yerkes' contemporaries in Chicago, but they were not successful on the District, largely because of the poor quality of the track, and they were replaced by traditional British designs within a few years. Despite this, the American influence on rolling stock design continued on the District. Most of the orders for new cars placed up to 1936 retained the American clerestory roof design and it survived until 1971, when the last of the clerestory-roofed cars, by then known as 'Q Stock', were withdrawn from passenger service.

The American influence on the District is exemplified here in the design of this 1903-built motor car. The car is one of a batch of 14 ordered by the Americans to provide two prototype trains before the main order. The cab end is enclosed while the trailing end is an American-style open entrance platform.

Even operations were Americanised, with the traditionally English 'up' and 'down' train directions being replaced by 'eastbound' and 'westbound', 'carriages' becoming 'cars' and 'bogies' becoming 'trucks'. Even drivers were replaced by 'motormen'. Many of these terms survive to this day, despite attempts in recent years by marketeers to eradicate anything related to railway language in the public consciousness.

Even before electrification, there were attempts to automate the District's traditional British manual signalling system. Increases in train services were pushing at the limits of manual signalling, and an automatic signal, operated by the passage of trains instead of by a signalman using a lever, was tried on the Hounslow branch in 1901. It was imported from the US (of course) and it was successful enough for a complete system of them to be tried on the Ealing & South Harrow Railway when it was electrified in 1903. This too was successful and the Underground adopted it for its new tube lines and for the electrification of the District Railway.

The train detection system used for the District's automation of signals was known as a track circuit, where a low voltage current passed through the running rails that was shorted out by the arrival of a train in the section. The idea was patented in 1872 by an American, William Robertson, and was installed on a number of US main line railroads over the following years.

A feature of the American designed automatic signalling was the use of compressed-air for moving signals and (later) points. It first appeared in the US in the 1880s. By the time the system arrived in London, it incorporated air-operated trainstops at signals and tripcocks on the trains, a system imported from Boston that would automatically cause a train to stop if it passed a signal at danger. It was the first automatic train protection system in Britain and was a major factor in the Underground's superb safety record. It is still in use on the manually operated lines of the Underground today, including the District.

A brand new 7-car set of 1905 Stock (later known as B Stock) seen on test on the line to South Harrow near Park Royal. A total of 60 of these train were ordered for the District's electrification.

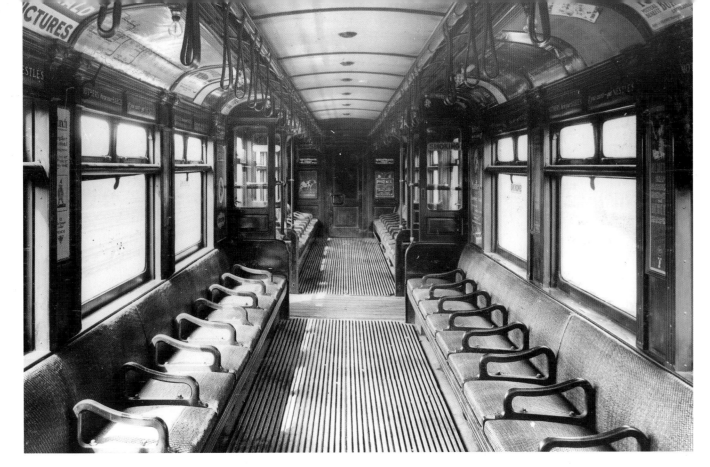

Above: Interior of American-designed District Railway B Stock car from 1905 with all-longitudinal rattan seating, providing a wide gangway along the car and plenty of the standing space needed for a rapid transit railway. Some of the cars in these trains had a mix of longitudinal and transverse seating.

Right: The interior of a C or D Stock car photographed in 1937 while cleaning is in progress. Of particular note is the classical architectural styling of the wood panelling, giving a much more homely style than in the 1920 (F) Stock that followed (see page 41).

Then and Now: WEST KENSINGTON c1905 AND TODAY

Then and Now: CHISWICK PARK c1910 AND TODAY

Promoting the District
Oliver Green

Looking back at the difficult early years of the District Railway it is not easy to explain how the company managed to survive at all into the twentieth century and become one of the key building blocks of the London Underground. Its financial position was insecure from the start and every attempt to grow and expand was difficult and uncertain. It was not easy to raise the capital to build the first section of line in the 1860s, and construction costs proved much higher than expected.

Partly because of this, expected amalgamation with the Metropolitan Railway was abandoned and the District was left out in the cold with an uncertain future. However the appointment in 1870 of the experienced railway manager James Staats Forbes as Managing Director, and soon afterwards Chairman, gave the company confidence that it could move forward effectively on its own. In fact the intense personal antagonism that developed between Forbes and his Metropolitan counterpart Sir Edward Watkin was nearly disastrous for both companies. While Forbes and Watkin were in charge, any co-operation or partnership between the two companies was highly unlikely, and yet without it the completion of London's 'inner circle' railway, which required at least some agreement between them, seemed doomed.

Because the cost of building in central London was so high, both underground companies looked for new opportunities to develop and grow by extending branches out of London and working in partnership with other railways. Watkin, with his plans to link the Met with other railways north west and south of London, was much more astute at this than Forbes. His grandiose vision included the creation of pleasure gardens at Wembley Park on the Metropolitan's Extension Line and even a rail link to Paris via a Channel Tunnel. On a more prosaic level he saw the possibilities for suburban housing development along the Metropolitan, though he did not see the full results of this in his lifetime.

At the District, Forbes and his colleagues did not seem to have a vision, or even a clear business plan, for the company's future. Always short of money, the District was much more opportunistic than the Met in its development strategy and would cut deals with other companies to allow expansion beyond the western suburbs, and later to the east. This was more likely to involve setting up separate companies or making through running agreements with others than getting further into debt through expensive infrastructure projects funded by the District itself.

Special edition of the District Railway Map of London published by Partingtons for Queen Victoria's Golden Jubilee, 1887.

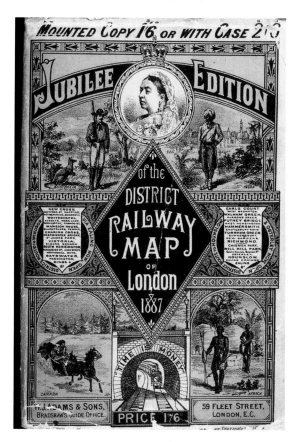

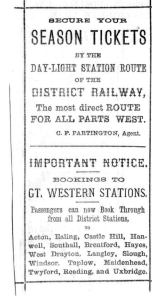

Extracts from a District Railway guide of 1873 (*top row*) and a London guidebook of 1887 (*below*), all produced by the Partington Advertising Company. These are fairly typical of railway advertising at the time, difficult to read and with a bizarre mix of typefaces that serves no useful purpose. Everything changed when Frank Pick took UERL publicity in-house from 1908.

In the 1870s and 1880s the District fanned out from the outer limits of its original line to serve many areas to the west and south west of London on short suburban branches, reaching Ealing, Hounslow, Richmond and Wimbledon. All these areas had bright prospects for suburban housing development and although the District did not get directly involved in this, as the Metropolitan was to do, increased passenger traffic soon followed the house builders.

Perhaps surprisingly, the District did not take the opportunity at this time to actively promote its growing suburban services through posters or print advertising. Railway publicity everywhere was still quite crude and unsophisticated in late Victorian Britain, and the District was no more advanced in this than the big main line companies. Its straightforward strategy, if it can be called that, was to contract this responsibility out to a London advertising agency, Partingtons, to manage on their behalf. The agency seems to have been given carte blanche to cover every available flat vertical space on the District's stations with commercial advertising, leaving little room for railway notices or even the station nameboards.

Overleaf: The District Railway Map of London, 1885. The company's own lines, along with the Inner Circle jointly run with the Met, are shown in thick red with other lines in blue. Where the District ran over other company tracks, such as the West London Railway, these are shown in red and blue together. It was the best map available but is still not entirely clear.

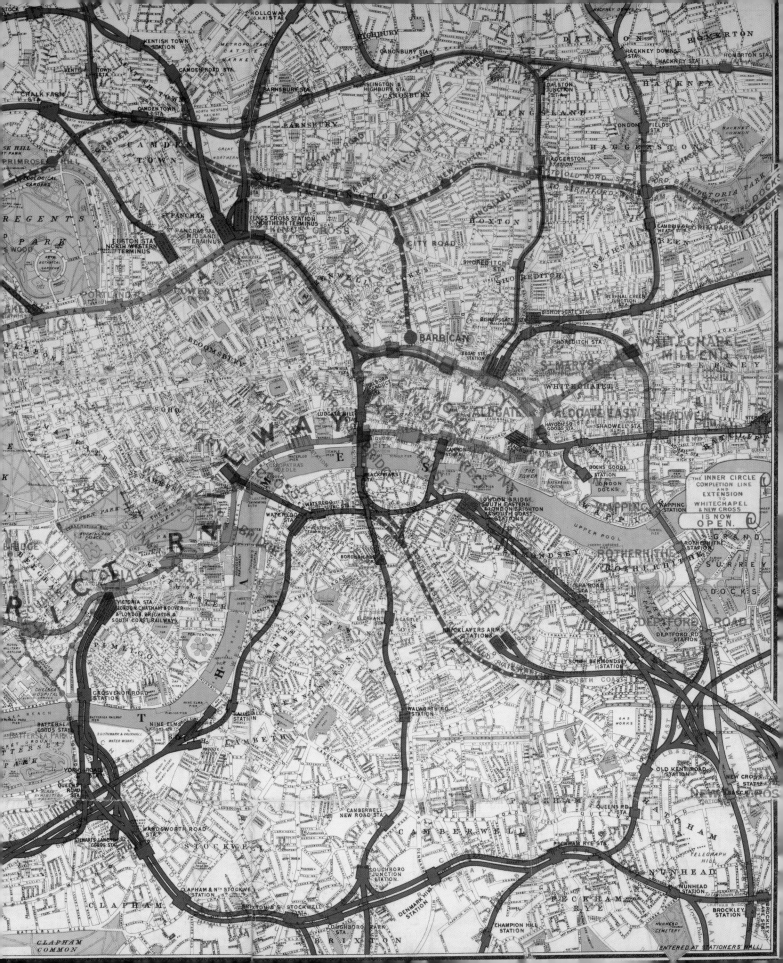

By the early 1900s the busy covered central London stations, worked by steam trains for over thirty years, were looking drab, grubby and visually chaotic. Both the District and the Metropolitan were regularly criticised in the press for the state of their underground stations and their unhealthy atmosphere but it was clear that neither would do anything about it until their lines were eventually electrified. Customer care was not a priority for the District until it began to face real competition in west London from smart, pollution free electric trams.

The one area where Partingtons did excel in promoting the District's brand was through maps. In the 1880s and 90s the District was well ahead of the Metropolitan and every other railway company in producing high quality folding maps of central London, which were updated with new editions every couple of years. The District's part of the Inner Circle and the western branches are shown prominently as thick red lines, with all other railways shown in thin blue, but this was the clearest railway map of London available at the time and obviously sold well to visitors and tourists.

Even if it seemed to ignore the interests of its regular passengers, the District was certainly alive to the benefits of attracting leisure traffic. Exhibition and entertainment centres were particularly important to the District as a major source of traffic, and the largest of these were created close to the railway's stations in west London. A series of changing exhibitions held on vacant land close to the Albert Hall attracted large crowds to South Kensington and in 1885 the District built a very expensive pedestrian subway from South Kensington station under Exhibition Road to the site: this is still used today, mainly by visitors to the museums.

After 1886, when the site was needed for the building of the Imperial Institute, the series of exhibitions was continued on District Railway land at Earl's Court. In 1894 London Exhibitions Ltd leased the Earl's Court site beside the line to develop it as an exhibition and pleasure ground. Among the attractions was the Great Wheel, based on a very popular and profitable feature of the 1893 World's Fair in Chicago. The London wheel, a similar attraction to the present London Eye, operated only until 1906, but the Earl's Court exhibition site continued in use for more than a century and is only now being redeveloped for housing.

The Great Wheel at Earl's Court, built in 1894 after the success of a similar attraction at the Chicago World's Fair of 1893. It was taken down in 1906 but the site, on District Railway land, was used for other exhibitions and entertainment for more than a century.

Just to the north of Earl's Court the vast Olympia building opened in 1886 and was also used for exhibitions and shows of all kinds. The District did not own the adjacent station at Addison Road (now Kensington Olympia) but was soon running services over the short link line from Earl's Court, as it does today. It is impossible to estimate the revenue benefit to the District of these local entertainment centres, but it is clear from the company's own financial reports that they considered the popularity or failure of annual shows to be the most important variable in their traffic figures.

But the unreliable benefits of 'leisure traffic' were never enough to make the District profitable. It suffered from what historian Charles E Lee has described in a Dickensian phrase as 'chronic impecuniosity' and, throughout its independent career, the District paid dividends on its ordinary stock on only five occasions. The highest distribution was just over 1% in 1880.

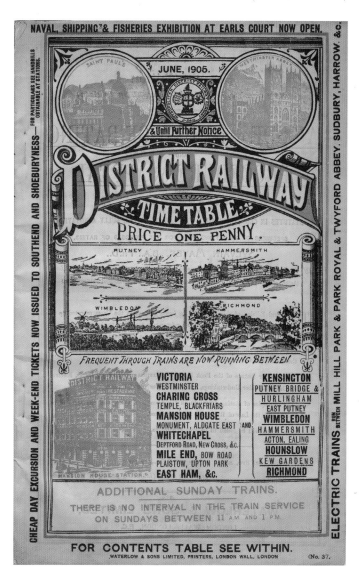

Above: District Railway guide to the Greater Britain Exhibition at Earl's Court, 1899.

Above right: District Railway timetable, June 1905. Lots Road power station was opened and by the end of the year all steam services had been withdrawn. Chairman Yerkes lived just long enough to see his Chicago-style electric trains in full operation, and died on a visit to New York in December.

The District was utterly transformed in less than five years at the start of the 20th Century by the massive injection of new American capital which provided complete electrification of the old system and the newly built extensions east and west. By the autumn of 1905 the District's smart new electric trains, painted maroon with gold lettering, were running right through London from East Ham to South Harrow. Suddenly, the railway's long held reputation for slowness, dirt and unreliability in the final years of steam was swept away.

Having successfully completed Yerkes' ambitious transit 'scheme' for London, the UERL now had to turn itself into a viable business operation. Although passenger figures were up, it soon became clear that neither the District nor the Tubes would be the profitable operations Yerkes had confidently predicted. In fact there was a real risk of bankruptcy unless the business was reorganised and found new ways to increase revenue income.

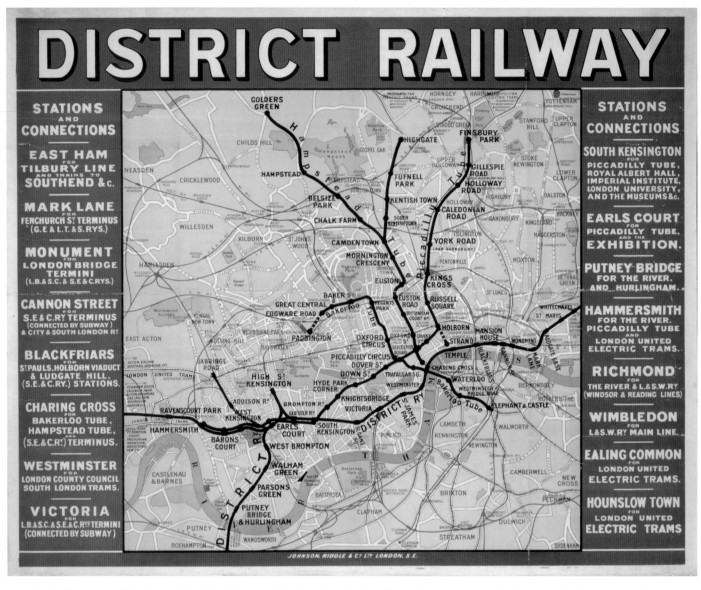

DISTRICT RAILWAY

District Railway map c1908 showing the UERL's three new Tube lines, the Bakerloo, Piccadilly and Hampstead Railways, which all opened in 1906-7 and had interchange with the District.

The saviour of the UERL was Albert Stanley, headhunted by the American directors from New Jersey, USA, where he ran the street railways (tramways). He came to London as general manager of the UERL in 1907, becoming managing director in 1910. Stanley quickly reshaped the management and operation of the UERL companies, engineering the takeover of the main bus company, the LGOC, a key move in the co-ordination of London's public transport services. He also put Frank Pick, who had joined from the North Eastern Railway in 1906, in charge of publicity, traffic promotion and development. Stanley, later Lord Ashfield, and Pick were to be the key figures in the creation of London Transport in 1933, when they became chairman and chief executive respectively.

The District Railway became the principal element of the UERL Traffic Combine, no longer an independent operation but benefiting from its enhanced and modernised role in the larger business. In the first five years after electrification, both passenger numbers and revenue receipts on the District were up by nearly 50%, a much faster rate of growth than on the Metropolitan or the new Tubes. When Pick started his publicity programme, using striking pictorial posters, new signage and free maps this marketing strategy covered all the UERL's operations and reflected careful attention to detail. The new system maps posted outside stations from 1908, the smaller pocket versions available free and many of the attractive new posters, used bold UNDERGROUND lettering in a distinctive typeface to announce themselves.

When the LGOC buses joined the UERL in 1912, new Sunday bus routes running from Underground stations took passengers on long excursions into the country, west to Windsor or south to Reigate. Pick took full advantage of the UERL's growing multi-modal road and rail network to make any journey by public transport look as simple and straightforward as possible, even where changes were involved. It was an astute marketing strategy and carried out with a panache that the Metropolitan and main line railway companies never quite achieved.

Stanley and Pick both understood that the UERL would never be a moneyspinner for shareholders but that it was important to develop a positive corporate image that emphasised the benefits of their services to London and Londoners. It was becoming increasingly clear that as London grew, the development and modernisation of public transport services was a growing factor in the change. The official statistics of 'rides per head' on Underground, bus and tram services show an astonishing increase of more than 50% between 1901 and 1911, the most intense period of electrification and extended rail services. Londoners were certainly 'getting the travel habit' as Edwardian newspapers were fond of calling it at the time.

The District was only one element of what Frank Pick liked to refer to as 'the framework of the town', the interlinked transport services that supported the life of the city. But it was a critical part, an important link that ran right across the city from east to west, providing core capacity that was supplemented by the new Tubes. Pick saw the potential for promoting it as a leisure line to all that London offered for work, shopping and entertainment in the centre but also as the gateway to London's countryside.

Pictorial posters to promote Underground leisure travel were first introduced by Frank Pick in 1908. This is a poster by maritime artist Charles Pears showing the pier and a sprit-sail Thames barge at Southend in 1915. Special through trains were available on the District, the only direct service to the seaside from the Underground.

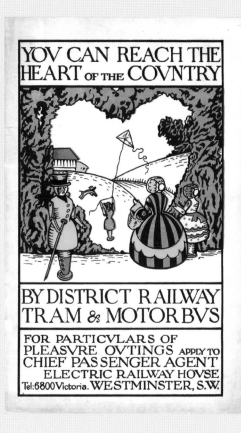

YOV CAN REACH THE
HEART of the COVNTRY

BY DISTRICT RAILWAY
TRAM & MOTOR BVS

FOR PARTICVLARS OF
PLEASVRE OVTINGS APPLY TO
CHIEF PASSENGER AGENT
ELECTRIC RAILWAY HOVSE
Tel: 6800 Victoria. WESTMINSTER, S.W.

PLEASURE OUTINGS
ON THE
DISTRICT RAILWAY.

Hullo! Did you come by UNDERGROUND?

APPLY TO THE PASSENGER AGENT'S OFFICE,
ELECTRIC RAILWAY HOUSE,
Telephone 6800 Victoria.   BROADWAY, WESTMINSTER, S.W.

T.O.T Supplement No.

PLEASURE OUTINGS
ON THE
DISTRICT RAILWAY

APPLY TO THE PASSENGER AGENT'S OFFICE,
ELECTRIC RAILWAY HOUSE,
Tel: 6800, Victoria.   WESTMINSTER, S.W.

THE DISTRICT RAILWAY
has specially catered for
PLEASURE PARTIES FOR CHILDREN
there are many resorts on its system where in
COUNTRY SURROUNDINGS
provision has been made for the comfort
and refreshment of large numbers. and
there is also the seaside at
SOUTHEND
the District Railway serves by itself and
its Underground connections almost every
quarter of London and waits to be of
service to you
SPECIAL CHEAP RATES
are quoted for parties for large numbers
(over 30 adults) and full particulars can
be obtained on application to
THE PASSENGER AGENT
ELECTRIC RAILWAY HOUSE
BROADWAY WESTMINSTER
S.W.

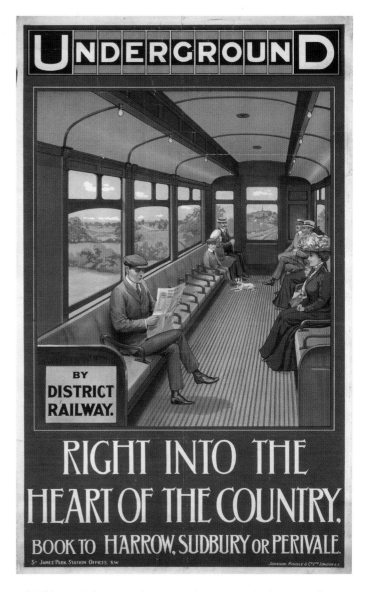

Opposite: The District offered special day excursion and party rates for families and children on 'pleasure outings' to London's country in the west and the seaside at Southend to the east.

Above: Two posters from 1909. The first publicises the Hounslow branch of the District for cheap fares and low rents for growing suburbs. The second promotes the use of the South Harrow line for country excursions.

The large, high capacity open saloons of the electric trains were ideal for taking organised party groups of city children up the western extension for a day in the country at Eastcote. In the other direction the link to the London, Tilbury & Southend Railway made it possible to run special excursion trains to the coast, swapping to steam locomotives for the unelectrified main line beyond Barking. This ability to promote direct access to the seaside by train from the Underground, which was unique to the District, seems extraordinary today. An even more popular day out by District was a trip to Kew Gardens, which became the most frequent individual subject of Pick's poster programme and the Underground's in later years. It is still the best way to get to get to Kew today from central London.

By the time the District Railway became part of London Transport in 1933, there was no need to promote and publicise it separately from the rest of the Underground. Nevertheless it has remained a distinctive and individual part of the network.

Riding on the District 1
Dr David Lawrence

In the first of two chapters looking at the trains used on the District Line over a period of almost 100 years, we look at the F Stock of 1920 to the R Stock built between 1949 and 1959. The railway car can be seen as an extension of the domestic interior – a moving room. It has four sides, some of which will have windows and doors; it has a floor and a roof; it has seating and lighting. Surfaces surrounding the passengers will have some form of decoration; this can be the plainest coat of paint, wood veneer or plastics, patterned textiles, leather, treated metal and rubber. Route diagrams, London Underground publicity and commercial advertising give a final embellishment in the way that prints or paintings might do at home.

Seating layouts have varied over time. There may be longitudinal bench seats facing each other along the car walls or a transverse arrangement where two benches for two passengers each are opposite eah other in a bay. Until recently there would be a mix of the two formats, but today the need to maximise standing space means that all District Line trains have longitudinal seating only. According to the fare paid, passengers had a choice until 1940 of First Class and Third Class (there was no Second Class in the period covered here) until First Class was abolished five months after start of the Second World War. First Class passengers had a slightly superior décor in their doored compartment and a much better chance of getting a seat in peak hours.

F Stock

We begin with the F Stock of 1920 as it marked a big departure from North American influences in the styling on London Underground vehicles. These trains would have appeared very modern indeed to the District Line passengers of the day. The interiors, however, were somewhat austere and within a few years had to be improved. Constructed mainly of steel, F Stock benefited from an increased width of seven inches over earlier designs and had a smooth curve to the roof in contrast to the clerestory roofs of most earlier District trains. Before 1923, partitions with swing doors separated cars into saloons for 'First' and 'Third' classes of travel. These were then superseded by arched part-screens without doors. The choice of steel for construction did not deter the District Railway from emulating the opulence of contemporary domestic interiors: walls and seat backs were treated using a technique called 'graining', where dark and light browns were applied to a more utilitarian base material and then textured to resemble the figuring of good-quality wood. Further references to the domestic interior are seen in the provision of opal glass dished lamp shades on cast metal brackets aligned with ornate metal grilles along the centre of car ceilings, and in the original choice of linoleum for the floors.

Designed for high-speed working, F Stock would feel lighter, faster and yet more solid than previous types. The oval end windows seem to have been in fashion at the time and, 70 years before the idea was used again, these windows were cut into both ends of every car, which along with the greater width, gave a spacious feel to these fine vehicles. They also included more longitudinal seating than their predecessors, or for that matter their immediate successors, helping to maximise space.

Opposite: District Line 1920 Stock, showing a big change from American styling that must have looked very modern compared to what had been built before.

Right: A trailer car of District Line 1920 Stock (later designated F Stock) showing the incandescent lighting, leather hand-grabs looped over rails, and both longitudinal and transverse seating. Vertical poles along gangways and the edges of longitudinal seats have supplemented the overhead loops and grab-handles on bay seat corners, but were found to be obstructive and removed during an alteration programme in 1923.

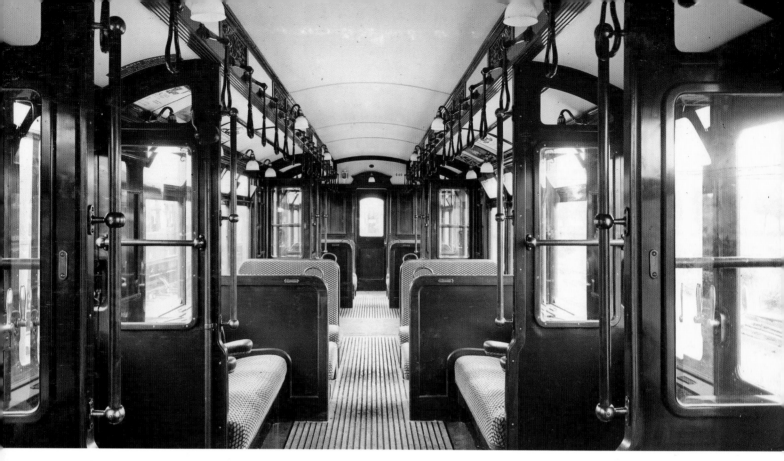

Interior of a 1923 G Stock car (later to become Q23) in original condition. The softer feel of the later American style interiors has returned as has the clerestory roof.

G/K/L Stocks

The next new District trains, the G Stock, were ordered just three years later and reverted to the American influence of earlier designs. This was because they were all motor cars designed to run with 1905 B Stock trailers, which themselves had been converted from motor cars and reclassified as H Stock. The clerestory roof returned with the G Stock and gave some similarity of appearance with the older stock it was to run with, but the frontal appearance was softened by having windscreens with gently arched tops. The stock also reverted to a width of 9ft, compared with the F Stock's 9ft 7ins. More transverse seats were fitted than on the F Stock and these seats were high backed, so in terms of passenger comfort – if not appearance - they marked some degree of improvement.

With the letter H used for the converted B Stock and the letters I and J not used, the next stock for the District was the K Stock of 1927. This was to enable the conversion of further B Stock motor cars of 1905 to continue in work as trailers. The trains of K Stock improved on the G Stock in having wider windows in the central bay of the car, but otherwise followed similar styling. Further trains were ordered for the District four years later. Externally very similar to the K Stock, inside there was much use of polished wood veneers and inlaying. They were the last of the trains built new for the District with clerestory roofs. The cars were mostly used to replace 1905 B Stock built as trailers but by the time the last of the L Stock entered service there were still 133 cars of wooden bodied B Stock in use, by then 27 years old. One priority of the new London Transport therefore was to look to the replacement of these. It should also be noted here that up to now all District trains had hand-operated passenger doors which would horrify today's Health & Safety people but was no different in this respect from the slam doors on, for example, the Southern Electric lines. London Transport wanted to convert all the cars it could to air-operated doors locked between stations, but even as late as 1936 new cars for the District were being built with handworked doors to work with older stocks.

Above: L Stock motor car number 700. We see moquette-covered longitudinal and transverse seating, light fittings and hand-grabs suspended from the ceiling, wooden flooring, and the wooden veneer finish to the car furnishings. The double entrance/exit doors are manually-operated, with handles both inside and out.

Right: A train of clerestory Q Stock seen alongside a North London Line train at Kew Gardens station in the 1950s.

Above: Two ladies alight from a Q38 Stock car just before the war. The flared sides of the body were also applied to the sliding doors.

Below: An O Stock train when new in 1937. All of these impressively designed trains were built with air-worked doors and were similar in appearance to the District's Q38 Stock trains which followed.

O and P Stocks

These two stocks were principally built for the Hammersmith & City line (O) and the Metropolitan line (P) but a few were used from the start on the District and in later life they were all used on it. They represented a big step forward in design that was used also for the District's next new trains, the Q38 Stock. A noticeable difference between the O and P stocks was that the former had high backed transverse seats and the latter low-backed ones. From the passenger's point of view there was little difference between individual cars of P Stock and Q38. However, whereas a P Stock train was made up of all new cars, the Q38 Stock was mixed with older, clerestory roofed, cars, to make up rather odd-looking trains.

Above: Mixed train of Q Stock in 1939 showing how badly the new Q38 cars mixed with the older flat sided and clerestory roofed cars. The curved front to the clerestory roofs in this train identifies the older cars as being from a later batch than the Q23 Stock leading car in the photo on page 43.

Below: Interior of a Q23 Stock car in final operating condition. The green and cream colour scheme had become standard on older stock. Much use is made of stained wood mouldings around windows and advertising panels. The London Transport Museum has launched an appeal to restore this Q Stock train to operational glory in honour of the 150th anniversary of the District Line. The train holds a pivotal place in London's social history, and had a role evacuating children to safety in the Second World War, and later for transporting spectators to 1948 Olympic venues. The Museum hopes to raise £150,000 to ensure the Q Stock can take to the tracks again. To donate and find out more about the project, visit www.donate.ltmuseum.co.uk/q-stock-restoration or call 020 7565 7442.

Q Stock

Reorganisation and some modernisation of District Line trains occurred not long after London Transport came into being in 1933. As part of a greater modernisation, the letter 'Q' represented several former classes converted or simply reclassified to run with newer vehicles. Stock classifications were Q23 (formerly 1923 G Stock), Q27 (1927 K Stock), Q31 (1931 L Stock), Q35 (M and N Stock, built 1935/1936) and Q38 Stock, built to complete the trains of older cars.

Interior finishes and fittings of the K, L, M and N stocks achieved some standardisation. Each had metal loop and leather strap hand grabs secured to the sides of the clerestory ceiling, with bracketed and shaded lamps at intervals. Above the grabs were ventilator grilles. Exploiting innovation in the toughening of glass, draught screens introduced an element of modernity by being frameless on their outside edges. Walls and seat sides in contact with seated passengers were of wood veneer with an inlaid lining. Lower sections of draught screens were painted. From around 1938 into the 1970s, a particular blue-green paint could be seen in Underground vehicles. Green was a traditional railway colour. It hides the dirt, whilst being both bright and calming: three important qualities for busy, often crowded spaces. Today's thinking is different.

Seating moquette design, which continues to bring colour to Transport for London vehicles today, was an extension of a tradition for patterns in upholstery textiles and wallpapers. From the 1920s, London Transport had selected both geometric and figurative motifs from artists including Enid Marx. Woven with wool, the moquette used will comprise a repeating image of dark, dirt-concealing hues, with brighter highlights for visual interest.

When G, K, L, M and N stock vehicles were converted into Q types, alterations gave some interior visual consistency with the new Q38 cars. Spherical rubber hand-grabs, suspended on spring-enclosed steel cables directly from castings attached to the clerestory sides, took the place of bracketed leather and cast metal loops from 1938. However, doors on some of the older types continued to be hand-operated until after the Second World War. The conversion to air doors began just before that war and continued until 1955.

Q38/R Stocks

Q38 Stock, which was built after O Stock but before P Stock, brought District Line travel forward into modernity once more, though it mixed with older stock on the line for another 33 years. It took interior details scaled-up from experimental tube stock of 1935, but with body sides flared outwards at the bottom to narrow the space between platform and train. Streamlining can be perceived too in the integration of straight lines and curves, and cylindrical and rectangular forms for seat bases and draught screens. O, P, Q38 and, later, R stocks all followed the same general design. The detail of interior fittings – including a vestigial clerestory – is unchanged from a decade earlier but the overall appearance is of a much more modern vehicle.

There are important developments also. Doors are now mechanically-powered, and actuated by passengers pressing buttons on the draught screens. Hand-grabs are mounted directly to the ceiling. Opening windows push outwards, between flared metal prisms. O, P and Q38 cars had tungsten lamps concealed by individual frosted glass shades of fluted 'art deco' form.

R Stock cars, which were built between 1947 and 1959, to a similar appearance to Q38 cars, had fluorescent strip lighting. This was also fitted to Q38 Stock cars that were converted to R Stock in the late 1940s. The 1947 cars were steel built, but from 1949 aluminium was used for the bodies of the new trains. The R Stock is remembered not only for its comfortable, deeply upholstered seats but also for its lateral rocking motion and the high-pitched tone of the motor generator. From 1953, R Stock began to appear in unpainted aluminium, making it look even more modern. For mixing in formations of older trains, these latter were painted silver or white to better match the newer cars.

Above: Interior of R49 Stock. Windows are large and unobstructed by framing. Fluorescent lighting is present, above the strip of advertising. The armrests are covered in imitation leather. At this time publicity officer Harold F Hutchison promoted the bar and circle brand mark for many uses: we can see it here on the line diagrams, for the 'No Smoking' transfers on the windows, and in the fabric pattern designed by Edmund Chapman at weavers John Holdsworth.

Right: In 1979 we see the final appearance of R Stock interiors. Wood veneer at seat backs and on draught screens has been supplanted by green paint, adding uniformity but also reducing distinction of surfaces. Furnishings look worn and dated in contrast to the D78 Stock which was soon to replace older vehicles.

Working on the District 2
Mike Horne

The creation of London Transport made very little difference to District staff beyond small changes resulting from the attempt to harmonise wages across the enlarged organisation. The men's representatives sought to cling onto concessions granted to District men from previous regimes, and some of these union agreements, mostly trifling, lingered on until the 1980s. Electric trainmen were first allocated to crew depots at Parsons Green, Acton Town, Cromwell Road (later closed) and East Ham but the meal reliefs were given at Sloane Square until transferred to Earl's Court in 1943. New crew depots were opened in the late 1950s at Barking (replacing East Ham) and Upminster.

A complication arose when London Transport assumed responsibility for operating stations along the Upminster line in 1969. These stations had always been operated British Railways, or its predecessors. Most existing staff were transferred to London Transport but they were given a choice whether to adopt London Transport or British Railways terms and conditions for the rest of their service, which was an administrative inconvenience. One new member of staff at Upton Park (one of the transferred stations) was Hannah Dadds, who later became a guard and then, in 1978, a train driver on the District. She was the first woman train driver on the Underground (previously, women had only been employed at stations but now all jobs are available).

In the 1980s and 90s there were profound changes to the way the District was staffed, resulting from initiatives affecting the whole system. The new D Stock trains, which entered service from 1980, had been designed with the possibility of conversion to one-person operation (OPO) in mind. After several years of union negotiation, this was introduced from 4 November 1985. Under this system, the driver (now styled Train Operator) operated the doors at stations. This required new rules and additional safety equipment to mitigate the effects of withdrawing the guard. The upgraded train radio much improved communication between train operators and the control staff, meaning drivers were no longer operating entirely alone with little idea of what was happening around them and in an emergency could summon help more quickly. The train operators received an increase in pay for the additional responsibility.

At about the same time ticket gates and new ticketing equipment were introduced reducing the pressure on manned ticket offices (displacing some booking clerks) and converting the long-standing role of ticket collector to gateline assistant. The District had been the first to trial a form of automatic ticket barrier at a number of stations between 1964 and 1967. Indeed there had been an experiment with a more primitive form of automatic gate at Westminster back in 1928 and this lasted about two years before it was abandoned.

Perhaps becoming a London Transport celebrity, Hannah Dadds is shown here in October 1978 shortly before qualifying as the Underground's first female train driver. Here a group of staff are being given technical instruction about train operation and fault finding on an R Stock train by a Trainman's Inspector. Hannah (whose sister, Edna, later also became a train driver) retired in 1993 and died in 2011.

Gates similar to those in use today were initially installed only in the central area but in the early 1990s they were extended throughout the line. Reorganisation of staffing in the early 1990s eliminated all the traditional station grades and their replacement by station assistants and station supervisors who could be used more flexibly. These staff were qualified, or licensed, only for the roles needed at the stations to which allocated, and could be multi-functional, doing different jobs at different times. This saw the end of booking clerks, no longer necessary as the accountancy function was now done by computer and fares simplification reduced the specialist knowledge needed. Further fares simplification and widespread acceptance of bank cards instead of cash allowed all station ticket offices to be closed in 2015/16, extra vending machines being installed if required. Station supervision once involved the perambulations of the ever-watchful inspectors, but with traffic growth and new technology, stations are now equipped with CCTV monitored from a fixed supervision point and at the larger stations from a dedicated control room. In only twenty years the way stations operated had changed probably more than in the previous one hundred.

From the early 1960s automation allowed concentration of most of the signalling supervision from local signal boxes to a control room at Earl's Court, with only three signal boxes still in operation in 2018 at the east end of the line. These were scheduled for imminent closure with signalling and train control becoming fully automated. An automatic train (using R Stock) was also tested in passenger service from April 1963 between Stamford Brook and Ravenscourt Park. These tests proved the equipment worked well enough to be introduced on the new Victoria Line but it did not immediately impact on District Line staff. Under London Transport control, the day to day operation of the District was delegated to a divisional control organisation based at Earl's Court, the management being shared with the Piccadilly Line (as, since 1932, train services interworked extensively). This arrangement endured until 1988, when, to strengthen management of the system, each line became a management unit in its own right. Naturally, the new managers were keen to differentiate the different lines and indicate to the public that local managers were now in charge. The District's users

quickly saw an explosion of 'District green' publicity, including a succession of leaflets and newsletters, highlighting what was going on. More importantly, the new line managers became fully accountable for line performance and from the early 1990s gradually acquired full responsibility for track, rolling stock and station maintenance (which had been centralised since the early 1920s). Certainly one impact of local managers 'taking control' was an increase in staff morale and improved staff relations.

District passengers mostly acknowledged that the new structure was improving ambience and service reliability but long-standing shortage of investment resulted in the government announcing in 1998 a public-private partnership to upgrade the trains, stations and equipment. Though not fully live on the District until 2003 it resulted in huge management reorganization and control of the assets passing to a private company called Metronet, to which District maintenance staff transferred. District operations (though remaining distinct) became part of the sub-surface group of lines with some loss of hard-won local control. Metronet collapsed financially in 2007 and control of maintenance transferred back to the Underground, though was never returned to the various lines.

The District Line is still a coherent management unit and is responsible for the daily operation of the trains and stations it serves. Stations are grouped into a number of areas with a manager in charge of each. Duty managers are always available throughout the traffic day and, on shift, each station is in the charge of a supervisor with customer service assistants and, where required, multi-functional staff. There may be more than one supervisor at the larger stations. Train operations have altered comparatively little with train operators (some qualified to train others) coming under the immediate control of a small number of duty managers (some detailed to manage operational incidents). Train operations are supervised by signallers and a service controller based at Hammersmith.

The District has come a long way in 150 years but despite all the new technology it is still dependent, each day, on hundreds of dedicated staff delivering a high quality public service.

Then and Now: ACTON TOWN c1895 AND TODAY

Then and Now: WESTMINSTER 1937 AND TODAY

The District in War
Mike Horne

When the Second World War broke out on 3 September 1939 it was inevitable that the District Line would be badly affected as its tracks ran on the surface – or just beneath – and the route through the City and the industrial areas of east London made it an unfortunate casualty of London bombing.

The District ran close to (and below) river level, so flooding was a particular worry – even a small breach of the Thames, or in one of the many feeder rivers that crossed the District, would cause widespread flooding and risk water getting into the tube network as well. The solution was to build several massive floodgates, one at South Kensington and one either end of Charing Cross (now Embankment). These comprised huge power-operated steel gates mounted in the tunnel roof that could be swung down to lock against a steel frame built into the tunnel, thus forming a watertight seal. The lower sill was designed to accommodate the running rails and small wedges were used to seal the flange-ways. By this means any inrush of water could be confined to a relatively small section of line. No gate was required east of Mansion House as the tunnels quickly rose to a level higher than river level. Signalling was interlocked with the gates and it was possible to run a limited train service when gates were closed as a precaution during air raids, the gates opening and closing for the passage of each train.

One of the earliest wartime tasks was the emergency evacuation from London of large numbers of people thought particularly vulnerable, including 607,635 school children who were to be billeted around the country in areas considered safe. This precautionary move began when war seemed inevitable but had not actually been declared, the children being moved between 1 and 4 September. This could only be achieved by train and hundreds of special trains had to be run, together with impeccable planning to ensure the right child was on the right train, disembarked at the right place and was

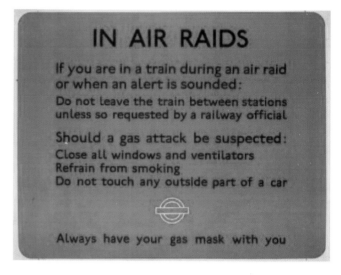

collected by the people who were expecting them. This massive task would have overwhelmed the London termini and the Underground was asked to help collect the children and take them to stations in outer London to make the necessary connections. The District had the job of collecting children living near its line and taking them (often by special train) to Ealing Broadway to connect with Great Western Railway specials which started there. To give some idea of the massive scale of this task, 101,000 evacuees passed through Ealing Broadway alone during those four days, together with their luggage, and on top of the usual daily traffic.

Early in the battle of Britain, on the night of 7 September 1940, heavy bombing in the East End caused damage at West Ham and near Campbell Road and major damage at Plaistow where a train was hit, causing considerable destruction. The bombing continued for days and on 9th September destruction rained down upon Monument, Aldgate East, Bow Road and Parsons Green. And so it went on, repair gangs being constantly at work and the railway generally being patched up within hours. Some bombing caused much longer shutdowns. Parsons Green to Earl's Court shut for a week, Charing

Left: A London Transport police woman assists at Ealing Broadway, through which large numbers of children were transferred from Underground to main line trains as part of the evacuation of vulnerable people from the capital at the outbreak of the Second World War.

Top: After many years of procrastination Sloane Square received a modern ticket hall and up escalators from 27 March 1940 (the escalators were useful as the station was particularly deep).

Below: Sloane Square station on 13 November 1940. The new booking hall, and connecting escalators, were completely destroyed in an air raid two days earlier. Perhaps surprisingly the all-over roof (the last on the District) was repaired and lasted until 1956. Many stations received slight bomb damage but were quickly repaired.

Cross to Mansion House two weeks (with a later one-week closure) and St James's Park to Sloane Square three weeks; but this overlooks the sheer volume of interruptions of up to a day or two and individual station closures of longer duration. Several sites were hit more than once, such as Whitechapel, which was very badly damaged.

Sloane Square ticket hall had been entirely reconstructed in the early days of the war, with up escalators linking each platform to the ticket hall from 27 March 1940. On 12 November 1940 the station building, ticket hall, staff canteen and new escalators were demolished by a 1500kg high explosive bomb, the wreckage falling onto the last coach of a departing train and destroying it. In all, 42 people were killed. The entire section of railway was closed for 12 days and a temporary station came into service from 2 December.

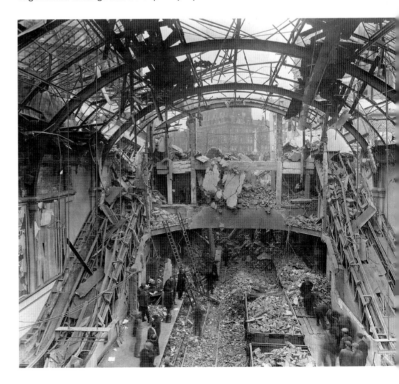

To try and protect stations from blast outside, many had blast walls built just beyond station entrances which did nothing for their appearance, but these were removed quickly after hostilities finished. In addition large signs were removed as a potential aid to enemy aircraft and lighting was reduced to support blackout requirements. Trains were blacked out by a combination of window netting (which also protected against glass splinters) and severely reduced lighting during air raids.

Trains were hit on a number of occasions and on one alone 70 cars were damaged when a land mine struck the depot at East Ham. Most cars were repairable but 11 had to be written off, including several new ones. One unusual 'repair' involved two of the new flair-sided cars which had each been badly damaged at one end. It was found possible to cut off the damaged ends and graft them together to produce one good car (this ran for several years with photographs of the repair work displayed inside).

Later in the War the V weapons began to cause new damage and further service disruption, and by 1945 the Underground was heavily patched up. The whole system suffered from heavily reduced maintenance caused by loss of staff to war effort, diversion of resources to cope with air raid damage, and difficulty in getting components and supplies; this began a maintenance backlog which lasted many years.

Most stations in the central area were provided with blast walls immediately outside; these were intended to protect those inside from nearby blast. The head office building above St James's Park received a direct hit on night of 14/15 October 1940 which seriously damaged the West Wing.

Above: Plaistow station received a direct hit from a high explosive bomb on 7 September 1940 and a District train standing in the bay platform was very badly damaged. The nearest car was written off but part of the second car was recovered and spliced together with part of another car, damaged during a separate raid, to form one good car.

Below: A high explosive bomb arrived at Turnham Green on Sunday 20 October 1940 demolishing most of a nearby house and badly damaging the station viaduct and a departing train. The damage to the station was typical of damage found on the system every day during the blitz and a whole organisation was set up to effect temporary repairs and get trains moving again.

The District's Lost Branches
J.E. Connor

Of the lines once operated by the District, two have been lost completely and another two transferred to the Piccadilly Line. The earliest to close was the short branch to Hounslow Town, which ceased operation in 1909. In the summer of 1880, the Hounslow & Metropolitan Railway had received authorisation to build a line linking Mill Hill Park (now Acton Town) with Hounslow Barracks (later Hounslow West). A year later, a Bill was deposited with a view of connecting this with the London & South Western Railway between Twickenham and Strawberry Hill. However, the LSWR objected and that scheme had to be abandoned.

Despite this, the company pressed ahead and started building part of the proposed connecting line, with work commencing in 1882. It branched off the line from Mill Hill Park at a spot known as Lampton Junction and continued for just 550 yards before terminating at Hounslow High Street.

It was substantially built and included a viaduct section comprising twenty arches. The branch was double track throughout and the station, which was named simply Hounslow, was provided with two wooden platforms and a brick main building. It was equipped with a coaling stage, engine pit and locomotive watering facilities, and opened on 1 May 1883.

At this time, work was continuing on the section to Hounslow Barracks which was single track west of Lampton Junction and opened on 21 July 1884.

During this year, the earlier station was renamed Hounslow Town, but with the line to Hounslow Barracks now fully operational, the branch became superfluous. The company therefore decided to close it and build a station on the new line at Heston-Hounslow (today's Hounslow Central) by way of replacement. This opened on 1 April 1886 and Hounslow Town fell into disuse from the same date.

This was not to be the end however, as the company had a change of heart and reopened the branch on 1 March 1903, providing it with two trains an hour, with more in the peaks. Four months later, the Hounslow & Metropolitan Railway was purchased by the District and an electrification scheme was announced.

In association with this, a new curve was to be constructed linking Hounslow Town with Hounslow Barracks. This was to have a ruling gradient of 1 in 106 and comprise a single track. At its western end it joined the main line at Kingsley Road Junction, but the curvature was so sharp that it had a permanent speed restriction of 8mph. It was also deemed unsuitable for steam locomotives, but this was no problem as it was electrically worked from the outset.

Electric services commenced on 13 June 1905, with trains to Hounslow Barracks running via Hounslow Town, where they reversed. They then continued on their journey by way of the new curve, thereby leaving the direct route linking Lampton Junction with Kingsley Road Junction without any public workings.

The old signal box was brought back into use and a Board of Trade inspection report of 10 June 1905 stated that it had been "*re-locked in accordance with the new Hounslow Curve.*" It also mentioned that "*an old crossover road at the platforms has to be pulled out*", but made no reference to the station itself. From the only known track-level photograph, it is apparent that one of the platforms had been shortened to a two-car length and although the other continued further, its London end was very narrow and presumably not for public use. The old station was never busier. From January 1909 the branch had a ten minute service of two-car electric trains which plied back and forth between Mill Hill Park and Hounslow Barracks.

Sadly Hounslow Town's new lease of life was to prove short lived, as the company decided to build a replacement station on the direct line, which became the new Hounslow Town on 2 May 1909. This time it was to prove permanent and in 1912 the site was redeveloped as a London General Omnibus Company garage.

Above: The exterior of Heston-Hounslow station seen in the early twentieth century with its street level building on the right. The station opened in 1886 and was rebuilt in 1912. It became Hounslow Central on 1st December 1925.

Below: Metropolitan District Railway 4-4-0T No 4 stands by the running-in nameboard at Hounslow Barracks at an unknown date. As built in 1884, the station was a very basic affair and comprised just a single platform. It was renamed Hounslow West in December 1925 and was enlarged four years later. In 1931, it received a new street level building, designed by Charles Holden.

An extremely rare view of the exterior of Hounslow Town terminus seen immediately after final closure. The entrance doors were locked and posters directed potential passengers to the replacement station, which opened as Hounslow Town on 2nd May 1909, but was renamed Hounslow East on 1st December 1925.

The other branch to close completely was also very short and stretched for a distance of just 1,232yds. It connected Acton Town with South Acton and carried passengers from 1905 until 1959. The line received Parliamentary Authority in 1878, but nothing happened until construction started twenty years later. It was intended to handle goods traffic and connected with the North & South Western Junction Railway at District Junction near South Acton. It opened for goods traffic on 15 May 1899 and was originally a single line, although the formation was wide enough for another track to be added at a later date if required. It was initially used by trains conveying materials for the Ealing & South Harrow Railway, which was then under construction.

The ESH line was operated by the Metropolitan District Railway from the beginning and, in 1902, it was announced that it was intended to run a service of electric trains linking South Harrow with South Acton. However, when these began operating the following year, the section to South Acton had not been electrified, so they terminated at Mill Hill Park (today's Acton Town) instead.

A couple of years later, on 13 June 1905, an electrified service was introduced between Hounslow Barracks and South Acton.

To accommodate this, a single platform was erected behind the up side of the NSWJR South Acton station. Technically, the newcomer was located on a through line, but it was always used as a terminus. It was separate from its next door neighbour and had its own entrance and ticket office. The platform was long enough to take a six-car train and, at its south western end, stood the station building. This was a fairly basic affair, constructed of wood and corrugated iron. It was protected by a canopy and included a waiting room together with toilets for both sexes. On the platform, beyond the building, was South Acton signal box, which had a mechanical frame containing fifteen levers, of which two were spare when opened in 1905.

The majority of the branch was on embankment, but there was also a 62ft steel bridge over Bollo Lane and a 42ft bridge above Palmerston Road. A second track was laid on the formation in 1905, but the station itself was only served by one. North east of the platform, the branch continued to its connection with the NSWJR, which was controlled by District Junction signal box.

The line proved useful for goods traffic, with both the London & North Western and Midland Railways having running powers over it. Eventually these workings ceased however and District Junction was severed. The second track was taken out of use from 14 February 1932 and was subsequently lifted. On 15 February 1932, the branch service was reduced to a shuttle, operating to and from Acton Town. With only one track surviving, the station signal box was of no further use, so it closed and was demolished.

Initially, the shuttle was worked by two-car sets or a single B Stock vehicle, which had been specially adapted for the purpose. Just prior to the Second World War however, two G Stock motor cars were converted so that they could be driven from either end and from then on the service was formed of one vehicle only.

The branch acquired the atmosphere of a backwater and became known by various nicknames. Some members of staff referred to the working as the 'Tea Run', because it was reputedly possible to get out and

The entrance to the single platform ex-MDR terminus at South Acton, with the North London Line (ex NSWJR) station of the same name adjoining on the right.

back before the messroom kettle boiled at Acton Town, whilst others knew it as 'The Pony' or 'The Ginnie'.

Sadly, the branch had become unremunerative and Sunday services ceased from 15 June 1958. London Transport announced its intention to close the line completely three months later and the last trains ran on 28 February 1959. The service remained very good to the end, but there was clearly a lack of demand.

Although only closed in 1959, colour photographs of South Acton LT seem to be uncommon. In this view we see one of the G Stock cars which had been converted for double-ended operation, along with a closure notice beneath the clock and the site of the second track on the right.

The other two lines lost to the District are still very much in use, but are now part of the Piccadilly Line network. The first of these to be transferred was the Ealing & South Harrow Railway which connected the District at Hanger Lane Junction just north of Ealing Common with South Harrow.

Trains began operating to Park Royal & Twyford Abbey on 23 June 1903, but could go no further as heavy rain had dislodged some of the earthworks. This was quickly remedied however and services reached South Harrow five days later. Trains were originally hourly, but were soon increased to run every thirty minutes.

Above: The rural nature of the area around Park Royal is very evident in this view, which includes directional signs to both the original station and a private road serving the Twyford Estate.

Right: The original station at Park Royal & Twyford Abbey was opened in 1903 and comprised two wooden platforms. It was located on the south side of Twyford Abbey Road and, as can be seen, the accommodation was fairly basic. This view, which was taken from the footbridge, shows a simple shelter on the left and the main building on the right. Although officially known as Park Royal & Twyford Abbey, the suffix does not seem to have appeared on MDR tickets. The station closed in 1931, when the present Park Royal opened about 30 chains to its east.

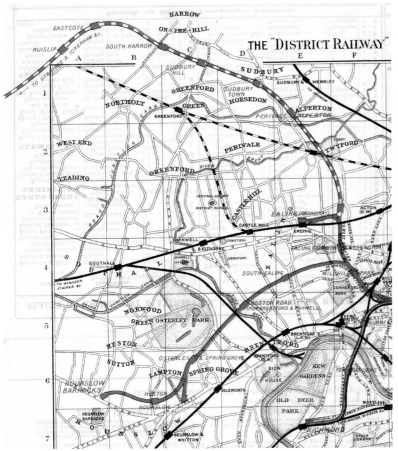

Above: Sudbury Town for Horsenden station on the South Harrow Line in its original form, photographed around the first decade of the twentieth century. It was rebuilt to a Charles Holden design in 1931 and was granted Grade II listed status forty years later.

Left: The western section of a District Railway map showing the routes serving South Harrow, Ealing, Hounslow and Richmond. At top we see the Ealing & South Harrow line, which was then under construction. The stations at North Ealing, Park Royal and Rayners Lane have not been included, whilst Alperton is shown in its pre-1910 form of 'Perivale-Alperton'. The old Hounslow Town terminus appears at the end of the short branch south-west of Osterley & Spring Grove, but the station itself is unnamed.

The line was extended beyond South Harrow to Rayners Lane Junction, where it joined the Metropolitan Railway route to Uxbridge, which opened in July 1904. A few District special trains ran over the connection in summer 1909, but regular District services did not start until 1 March the following year. During 1910, a siding was provided near South Harrow to serve the Harrow & Stanmore Company's gasworks. A crossover and signal box were also installed and these, along with the siding, were located to the north of Northolt Road. From 4 October 1910, a Metropolitan Railway steam locomotive would regularly propel a daily train of coal wagons into the works from Rayners Lane and return with a load of coke.

The basic service on the ESH line continued to improve and in January 1915 a morning business train was introduced linking South Harrow with Mansion House. It took thirty-nine minutes to complete the journey and was officially known as The Harrovian, although staff referred to it as 'The Pansy'. There was never a comparable evening working travelling in the opposite direction, but the morning fast train survived until the introduction of tube services.

In readiness for these, the old Park Royal & Twyford Abbey station was closed from 6 July 1931 and replaced by new premises to its east. The new station, which was named plain 'Park Royal', opened with temporary buildings, and was not completed until March 1936. All of the other stations along the line, except North Ealing, were rebuilt in connection with the forthcoming changes, but these invariably remained on their original sites. The one minor exception was South Harrow, which was partially resited to provide a better positioned entrance on the main road on 5 July 1935.

Piccadilly Line trains had reached South Harrow on 8 February 1932, although at first these only shuttled to and from Acton Town. Central London through services followed a few months later on 4 July, when District services ceased, and were extended at their western end to serve Uxbridge on 23 October 1933. The coal trains between Rayners Lane and the South Harrow Gasworks continued for two more decades, but finally ceased when the works closed on 4 April 1954.

The other part of the old District system to become part of the Piccadilly Line was that serving Hounslow referred to earlier. Full tube services began operating between Acton Town and Northfields on 9 January 1933 and were extended over the whole length of the route two months later, on 13 March. In connection with this, Northfields station had been resited in 1932, with Osterley following in 1934. For a little over three decades the route was served by both District and Piccadilly Line trains, but this changed from 10 October 1964, when it became Piccadilly only.

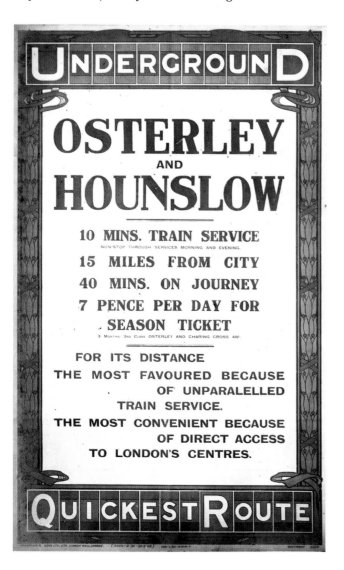

UNDERGROUND

OSTERLEY
AND
HOUNSLOW

10 MINS. TRAIN SERVICE
NON-STOP THROUGH SERVICES MORNING AND EVENING.

15 MILES FROM CITY

40 MINS. ON JOURNEY

7 PENCE PER DAY FOR
SEASON TICKET
3 MONTHS 3RD CLASS OSTERLEY AND CHARING CROSS 48/-

FOR ITS DISTANCE
THE MOST FAVOURED BECAUSE
OF UNPARALELLED
TRAIN SERVICE.
THE MOST CONVENIENT BECAUSE
OF DIRECT ACCESS
TO LONDON'S CENTRES.

QUICKEST ROUTE

Left: A poster advertising the benefits of living in the Hounslow area and using the Metropolitan District Railway for the daily commute into central London. In 1909, two-car electric trains began to run at ten-minute intervals, linking the branch with Mill Hill Park (Acton Town) where they connected with services to and from the City.

Above: The entrance to Northfield Halt (Ealing) on the west side of Northfield Lane. As can be seen, it was a very basic affair with a simple ticket hut and stairs leading down from the bridge. Access to the westbound platform is just visible on the left, whilst the entrance to the eastbound side is on the right, adjoining the hut.

Below: The exterior of South Ealing station at an unknown date, possibly around 1910. South Ealing opened with the original stretch of line between Mill Hill Park and Hounslow in May 1883 and had a street level building similar to those at Boston Road and Osterley & Spring Grove. It remained standing until 1931 when in was demolished and replaced by a temporary entrance. The 'temporary' street level building was not replaced by a permanent structure until 1988.

Signalling on the District
Thomas Crame

In common with the Metropolitan Railway which preceded it, the District utilised the common technology of the mid-Victorian era; mechanical lever frames with telegraph links between adjacent signal cabins. Like the Met, the District originally used block instruments to the design of C. E. Spagnoletti, who was the Telegraph Superintendent for the Great Western Railway and who worked as a consultant to both companies.

During the 1880s the original Spagnoletti instruments were replaced with ones to a design by W. R. Sykes. This design incorporated electrical interlocking between the block instrument and the lever frame. Sykes was also concerned with improving the operation of signals, including a trial of an electrically-actuated signal at Victoria.

As could be expected for the growing railway, there were a great number of alterations in the early years associated with extensions, track layout changes, and varying traffic needs, though a major factor for the development in the District's signalling practices was the electrification of the railway in 1905. This resulted in the introduction of what was referred to as 'power' signalling, which was to become a standard of both the District Railway and the early 'tube' lines such as the Piccadilly, and latterly, of London Transport. A number of the features of these initial power installations are recognisable on the District Line today.

The line was equipped with track circuits throughout, using a direct current circuit design and two polarised relays. Semaphore signals remained in the outside sections, and also for starting signals at stations in tunnels, but they were fitted with an air motor and an electro-pneumatic valve which was connected to an air pipe which ran between electrical substations. In the tunnels themselves, an air operated spectacle plate moved coloured lenses in front of an oil or gas lamp.

The 1906-1931 signal cabin at Hammersmith. The diagram shows the original layout with the District Railway at the top, and the terminating platforms for the Piccadilly tube to the bottom. The 39 lever Style B frame was split into two sections, for each railway, and featured key features introduced by the District including the drum train description transmitters to the centre and right of the frame.

To ensure that a train passing a signal at danger would be brought to rest, all signals which passenger trains encountered were fitted with an electro-pneumatically operated train stop. Points were also moved by compressed air, controlled by electro-pneumatic valves. Signal cabins had frames with miniature levers and illuminated diagrams showing track circuit occupancy, with the first in the world installed at Mill Hill Park (Acton Town today).

Signalmen were advised of the destination of an approaching train by means of the diagram, using combinations of four wires to give different 'Train Descriptions'. This system was simple, but effective - some components of it remained in use until 2012.

One name that is synonymous with the development of London Underground's signalling is Robert Dell (1900-1992). Joining the District Railway in 1916 as an Apprentice, he rose to become London Transport's Chief Signal Engineer. Dell's career owed a lot to a chance meeting in 1920 with William Every, the District's signal engineer, at Earl's Court. Every remembered Dell, who had won a prize for Best Apprentice, and immediately offered him a job in the signal drawing office.

Developments on the District followed a steady pace along with developments on the 'tube' lines, with technical improvements such as the conversion of DC track circuits to AC, and the introduction of enclosed trainstops to aid maintenance. However, Dell's vision was for increasing automation as an aid to reducing staff numbers and the period between 1932 and 1974 saw progressive developments in this regard. A large scheme was commissioned during 1936 which centralised the control of signal cabins at Cromwell Road, Earl's Court (East and West) and High Street Kensington into one cabin at Cromwell Road, which used route setting levers rather than individual levers for points and signals.

Dell's drive towards automation progressed, with the next step to separate the signalman from the levers themselves. A trial installation at Ealing Broadway in 1952 used a console with internally illuminated push buttons to control whole routes, with telephone type relays (similar in size to a modern smartphone, but significantly heavier) converting the operation of the button into commands for air valves to move the levers in the correct sequence. The power frames were redesigned, relocated in equipment rooms and renamed 'Interlocking Machines'. This combination was used at the eastern end of the District Line, where two tracks between Campbell Road Junction and Upminster were allocated for the sole use of London Transport, who installed its own signalling, controlled from two push button cabins at Barking and Upminster respectively.

Cromwell Road cabin 'EC', commissioned in 1936, featured 83 levers and controlled Earl's Court, Triangle Sidings, High Street Kensington and Gloucester Road. This was one of Dell's early signal cabins featuring route levers, rather than the previous practice of controlling signals and points by separate levers. Separate point levers were provided for emergency use, but it was not intended for them to be frequently operated.

The next stage of development was to remove the need for the signalman to have to operate the push buttons, concentrating them in one place and leaving them to supervise rather than signal trains. The device for automatically setting routes was known as the 'Programme Machine', introduced on the District Line in 1960. This contained the timetable on a roll of plastic film, with punched holes in a code format, which was read by the machine and used to initiate the operation of the signal and point levers.

The drawback of Programme Machine control was the complexity of the control circuitry associated with it. Early sites used relays, but in order to improve reliability (and save space), the circuitry was redesigned using diode logic circuit modules, which are still in use today. The first trial of Diode logic to control the levers on the interlocking machines was undertaken at Hanger Lane Junction in 1961, and this progressed to become the standard from the mid-1960s until the 1980s.

Much had changed by the time the District celebrated its centenary in 1968. The 1936 route setting installation at Cromwell Road had been replaced, first with push buttons in 1957, and then converted to Programme Machine working ten years later. The line from Ealing Common to Tower Hill (excluding West Kensington East and Mansion House) was controlled by programme machines from a new Regulating Room at Earl's Court, opened in 1965. The District had also hosted the first trials of Automatic Train Operation in London; initially on the test track at South Ealing (then shared with the Piccadilly line) and then an in-service trial between Stamford Brook and Ravenscourt Park during 1963.

Into the 21st century, the District Line continued to soldier on with its 1950s and 60s-era technology; however, plans for other rail projects required change. Construction of a new centre siding between Plaistow and West Ham commenced in 2010, with a new relay interlocking interfacing with the Plaistow Interlocking Machine from January 2011. This allowed remodelling work to commence at Whitechapel, where the layout of four platforms and a siding (which had altered little since the early 1900s) was reduced to two platforms and two crossovers. Various other signalling works have taken place to support track renewal, particularly at points and crossings where the old electro-pneumatic point mechanisms are being steadily replaced with electric point machines.

Earl's Court Regulating Room, opened in 1965 and photographed some time after control of Putney Bridge and Parsons Green had been added in December of that year. The Regulators are sitting at desks which were more like office furniture than later control desks, with the majority of their controls being 'Winkler' switches for train descriptions. Later alterations moved the route buttons from drawers beneath the diagram to purpose-built desks which remain in use today.

Between 2012 and 2013 various signalling modifications were installed to support the introduction of the new S7 Stock fleet, and various track layout alterations were undertaken in readiness for resignalling as part of the Four Lines Modernisation programme; most notably the removal of the bay platform and crossovers at Putney Bridge, which allowed the westbound road to be returned to its pre-1910 position, the removal of the by-then disused stabling sidings at Ealing Broadway (which, incidentally, lost its crossover to the Central Line in 2011), and the installation of a new crossover at Earl's Court at Christmas 2016, reinstating one which had been removed when the area was resignalled in 1966.

The main challenge for the District Line in the next few years is the replacement of the current fixed block signalling system with a Communications Based Train Control (CBTC) system, provided by Thales. This will extend throughout the line. On the sections the District Line shares with the Piccadilly Line and Network Rail, it will either be 'overlaid', where the existing signalling will control the CBTC system, or 'underlaid' where the CBTC system will also control new fixed signals for manually driven trains.

The CBTC system uses trackside tags to give a position reference to trains, which communicate their position via a radio link. A pair of computer systems on the train are responsible for the implementation of Automatic Train Protection and Automatic Train Operation.

Fourteen Vehicle Control Centre (VCC) computers will be provided for the entire Sub-Surface network. These receive the train position information, evaluate the distance the train is permitted to travel, and send commands back to the train. The VCCs also provide the interlocking between routes and control the movement of points and other trackside equipment via an element controller. The new CBTC system will be controlled from a new Control Centre at Hammersmith and will enable the final closure of Earl's Court Regulating Room, the 1907 vintage signal cabin at Whitechapel and the facilities at Barking and Upminster.

Earl's Court Regulating Room from the outside, built above the Warwick Road entrance to Earl's Court Station. The subsequent Northern and Victoria line room at Euston was built on similar principles, but with a number of improvements, including both a larger room and a false floor to ease access to equipment.

Riding on the District 2
Paul Moss

Trains known as C77 Stock were ordered for the District Line Edgware Road to Wimbledon service and began to arrive in 1978 as the line's first new trains for some time. These had been a follow-on from virtually identical trains supplied eight years earlier for the Circle Line, where it had been considered that a 'people mover' configuration with four sets of double doors per car would assist rapid entry and exit for the short distances between station stops, particularly at peak times. All the seating was transverse which allowed increased standing room in the doorways.

London Transport's Design Consultants (Design Research Unit) had no input during the development of these trains and it showed. DRU were in their day Britain's leading design consultancy and headed by Misha (later Sir) Black who had done wonders to revitalise the image of British Rail including their inspirational double arrowed symbol. However they were totally sidelined by a cosy duopoly between LT's development engineers and their counterparts at Metro-Cammell.

The C Stock was a major contrast to the CO/CP/R trains that continued to run for another ten years on the rest of the District Line. These earlier train types had excellent through car visibility, but on the new trains seating was enclosed by draught screens that effectively 'walled off' the interior into separate 'cells'. The interior colour scheme was made up of pale blue-grey melamine laminates with satin anodised extruded aluminium sections; the seats being covered with a blue and green moquette designed by Marianne Straub which harmonised well with these colours. The transverse bulkheads carried illuminated advertising panels.

Right: C77 stock as new (top and centre) and towards the end of its life in original condition (right). The graffiti menace (here scrubbed out on the doors) affected all trains on the Underground and led to graffiti resistant paints being used on the refurbishments.

Time was not kind to this interior design, the seat pattern did not disguise worn and grubby surfaces well and the lighting tubes behind the advertising frames were rarely replaced when broken. They looked dirty because of a build up of dust in the corners and the rubberised panelling covering the heaters would peel away and often be left in that state showing adhesive marks. To make matters worse these trains were particularly badly hit both inside and out by the graffiti menace of the late 1980s. They appeared hostile and threatening, particularly for women passengers travelling alone from the late evening onwards. They seemed to be the outward expression of a weak management no longer in control of their assets.

Following the King's Cross Underground station fire in November 1987 the money was soon found to carry out an all-embracing and thorough fire safety programme across all aspects of the network, including the materials used within the trains themselves. All hazardous materials such as the melamine phenolic panelling (which gave off toxic fumes when alight), and even the time honoured ribbed maple wood flooring, were to be replaced by new interiors that would meet the very highest standards of fire safety achievable.

The C Stock trains were completely stripped out to a bare shell and the interior replaced by an exemplary design by Cre'Active Design Consultants; this was everything that the original solution was not. Using a now standardised two pack painted ivory colour colour scheme, on entry they at once appeared bright and welcoming, fully glazed draught screens coupled with longitudinal seating throughout the car provided exceptional visibility throughout the vehicles' length. Together with the addition of car end windows, the perception of a safe and secure environment was at last achieved. New flooring made in a composite rubber material replaced the wood and the new seats had a cheerful moquette design that reflected the three lines on which the C Stock operated. Vertical grab poles in the seating areas were added and were a useful and convenient addition for passengers, particularly in crush loaded conditions. These trains ran in service on the District Line's Edgware Road to Wimbledon service until their withdrawal between 2012 and 2014.

The transformation of C Stock achieved by Cre'Active Design Consultants in the 1990s.

The D Stock

Seventy five of these six car trains were ordered from Metro-Cammell. They were the longest on the entire Underground system and they replaced the rest of the old CO, CP and R Stock trains on the line between 1980 and 1983. This time around, the Design Research Unit was fully involved from the very beginning in their development and the results spoke for themselves. The heavy browed look of the former trains was replaced by DRU's "high forehead" style (as specified on their classic 1967 and 1973 tube trains). The cars were 60 feet in length with four sets of single leaf doors per vehicle. Originally left in their unpainted aluminium finish, they were simple yet elegant and well proportioned in appearance with sheer body sides as wide as possible at floor height but with a slight taper to the roof. This treatment was very much in the then DRU design idiom.

The interior design was a tremendous step forward and pre-empted that of the refurbished C Stock in several aspects. First the draught screen framing was commendably low, allowing excellent through car visibility as well as promoting an open and airy aspect. The overall colour scheme was bright and welcoming, using flecked oatmeal coloured laminates accented by the then fashionable colours of brown and pale orange. Misha Black's personal contribution was the moquette seating design that featured four colours – mustard yellow, orange, brown and black in a 'stacked bricks' format. Seating was in the main longitudinal with four sets of transverse seats in the car centre. Conveniently placed vertical grab poles in the middle of these seating areas were also a greatly appreciated feature of these vehicles.

Fitted for the first (and last) time on surface stock trains were 3.5ft wide single leaf doors as opposed to the traditional double doors. Adjacent to these, illuminated passenger-controlled door-open buttons were fitted when the trains were new. All in all when compared to the original C Stock vehicles, these were extremely pleasant trains in which to travel; all of the design elements such as the lighting troughs, ventilation grilles and the framing of line diagrams and advertisements being particularly nicely resolved.

Refurbishment of the D Stock

Because the fire safety performance of the original interior was still very good, there had not been the same pressure to change it as had been the case with all of the other train types. Being at that time the most modern trains in the fleet, they were certainly a "hard act to follow" because the starting point was still a very accomplished solution.

The design company Jones-Garrard was appointed back in 1996 to prepare concepts for a redesigned interior, but it was not until September 2000 that a prototype vehicle was produced. In the spring of 1999, London Underground had asked Cre'Active Design Consultants to 'engineer' a final interior design whilst maintaining the spirit of Jones-Garrard's work as closely as possible, and three prototype vehicles were produced. However it was found that many of the features could not be afforded because of budgetary constraints and so a reduced cost approach was taken.

Apart from being a visual update, very important improvements and additions for passenger safety and convenience were incorporated. Most important of these was the fitting of car-end windows and a multi-purpose area with tip-up seats was provided for wheelchair users. CCTV surveillance cameras were discreetly housed with a commanding view of the entire interior. The previous strap hangers were replaced by horizontal handrails with a gently undulating profile that had survived from the original concept sketches. Dot matrix 'next station' describers were located laterally throughout the car and similar electronic train destination displays were fitted behind car windows adjacent to the doors. The draught screens with their neat exposed fixings, ceilings and ventilation grilles remained unaltered.

Bombardier Transportation carried out the work throughout 2005 but by 2015 the trains started to be withdrawn with the final one gone in April 2017. They would be replaced by their successors some 15 years before their intended lifespan. A deal was struck whereby 150 driving motor cars and 70 trailers were bought by Vivarail to become BR Class 230 trains and converted to either diesel electric or battery electric propulsion.

Opposite page, top: D stock train when new.

Opposite page, centre: The single leaf doors.

Opposite page, bottom: The warm and inviting interior of the original D Stock trains.

This page, above: All of the refurbished D Stock trains were painted in this 'corporate' livery as were refurbished C Stock.

The refurbished interior design that went into production.

'S' Stock trains

New trains started to operate on the line in June 2014 and by April 2017 had completely replaced their predecessors. Built by Bombardier Transportation in Derby, they were part of a huge order for 191 trains with a value of £1.5 billion, arguably the largest single rolling stock order ever placed in Britain.

For the first time in the Underground's history, an essentially 'one size fits all' design is used on all of the sub-surface lines.

Designed by the in-house Industrial Design team, they represent a dramatic improvement over all previous stock types; in fact they are light years away from what was offered to the public to travel in compared to forty years ago when the 'C' stock appeared. Their outward appearance is a completely new, non-derivative design approach with a very sculptured frontal styling featuring curved glass blended with a very attractive 'tumble-home' to the extruded aluminium car bodies.

The interior design is even more dramatic with the ivory body colour again providing a bright and welcoming ambience. Safety, security and the well-being of passengers are a key part of the design concept. Fully open through car gangways give remarkable through car visibility and allow passengers to safely move from one crowded car to another.

A floor height level with the platform edges means that disabled passengers can easily enter and exit and each vehicle has a designated multi-purpose area with tip-up seats for wheelchair users and pushchairs. This is separated in their centre by a backboard with its own offset curved handrail to aid wheelchair manoeuvrability. Seating is cantilevered out from the wall surfaces to aid cleaning and the storage of small bags; this enables passengers to walk unimpeded throughout the cars. A standardised seat moquette pattern is fitted, using all the colours of the lines that S Stock serves.

For the first time ever on an Underground train air conditioning is provided, especially welcome in the summer months. Within the cars full passenger information is provided with transverse dot matrix indicators that show destination and confirmation of the line; these messages are also repeated on the train exterior. Finally after a long absence from Underground trains a number of yellow strap hangers were reintroduced.

These superb trains will supply all of the District Line's rolling stock needs until most probably the middle of the 21st century. Their design excellence will surely meet passengers' requirements well for the whole of the time they are in service.

Between 2014 and 2016 the District's D Stock was retired and replaced by new high-tech S Stock trains (shared with all the sub-surface lines). This interior view clearly shows the multi-purpose area.

Above: This 7-car S Stock train pulls into Chiswick Park (now a listed building). The large verdant space between the tracks is where the former District eastbound platform was situated before alterations in 1932 to accommodate the Piccadilly Line extensions from Hammersmith.

Below: Strap hangers make their return.

Station Design
Kim Rennie

As befits the second-oldest line on the Underground, the District Line has a wide variety of station architecture with examples of almost every design genre and decade. Gloucester Road is one of the oldest stations still in use with much of the original District Railway (DR) surface building surviving and dating from 1868. West Brompton is another example of an original DR station and from a year later. A distinctive feature is the large wooden trainshed over part of the platforms. Similar roof structures from the 1870s and 80s remain at Earl's Court, Ealing Broadway and Fulham Broadway. Pre-WW1 DR surface buildings survive at Barons Court, Ealing Broadway, Fulham Broadway and Temple, though only two remain in railway use. Other early stations include Kew Gardens, Stamford Brook and Ravenscourt Park; which are of L&SWR origin from the 1860s.

Harry Ford's 1905 ticket hall at Barons Court showing the original full-height tiling in shades of green and decorative faience blocks used as surrounds to the booking office windows.

Above: Bow Road is one of two surviving stations opened by the Whitechapel & Bow Railway in 1902. The single storey structure is of red brick and attributed to engineer C A Brereton. As built, these stations had separate entrances and exits and the former, long disused, can be seen on the left.

Below: Earl's Court was rebuilt in 1906 by Harry Ford to accommodate the Great Northern, Piccadilly and Brompton Railway (today's Piccadilly Line). Work included a new façade on Earl's Court Road faced with a light-brown tiles, green keystones and a green frieze bearing both the DR and GNP&BR names in white. The replica 'heritage' detailing has been fitted to the entrance canopy in recent years.

The Wimbledon branch retains almost all of its stations from the 1880s. Wimbledon itself is an exception, being reconstructed by the SR in the late-1920s and including a Portland stone façade.

The turn of the 19th Century saw the Whitechapel & Bow Railway open in 1902 and Bow Road and Stepney Green remain in generally original condition. Earl's Court gained its attractive Harry Ford frontage in 1906, the same year that the opening of the GNP&BR (today's Piccadilly Line) saw classic Leslie Green ox-blood designs added to Gloucester Road and South Kensington. During the same period the LT&SR rebuilt East Ham, Upton Park and Plaistow stations to accommodate DR traffic and these survive mainly intact.

St James's Park station was rebuilt in 1929 in connection with the construction of the Underground headquarters at 55 Broadway above.

The District Line has a number of classic 1930s Charles Holden stations. Ealing Common shares a design concept with Hounslow West (both of 1931) in having a heptagonal tower in Portland stone. Acton Town (1932) is a development of the Sudbury Town brick 'box' built for the Piccadilly Line extensions of the time. Chiswick Park (1932) displays some similarity with Arnos Grove, though the ticket hall is not a complete 'drum'. West Kensington is a more modest Holden design from c1927.

The extension of regular District services from Barking to Upminster in 1932 and associated four-tracking led to new or rebuilt stations being provided by the LM&SR at Upney, Becontree, Dagenham Heathway (then Heathway), Dagenham East (then Dagenham), Hornchurch and Upminster; with Elm Park and Upminster Bridge added shortly afterwards. These are

Ealing Common, from 1931, is one of the most distinctive stations on the Underground. Design is by Adams, Holden and Pearson, with assistance from Stanley Heaps. The exterior is clad in Aberdeen granite up to door height and Portland stone above. The heptagonal ticket hall tower originally carried an enamelled name frieze, now replaced by ceramic tiles.

The reconstruction of Mile End in association with the eastern extension of the Central Line was a pre-war project delayed by hostilities and finally completed in 1946. The entrance building was designed under Stanley Heaps's supervision and marked a return to the simple Portland stone screen concept first devised by Holden in the 1920s. The exterior is now unusual in retaining a reference to 'London Transport'.

mostly similar in construction combining dark red brick, metal window frames and single storey street-level elevations.

Mile End was rebuilt in 1946 to accommodate the eastern extension of the Central Line. The entrance has a Portland stone screen whilst at platform level there are numerous tiled support pillars suggestive of the New York Subway.

The period from the late 1940s to the 1980s has given us no buildings of great note, the only major construction being the rebuilding of Barking by BR in 1959-61. Tower Hill was provided with a new entrance in 1988 that allowed the cramped 1967 ticket hall to become exit-only. The roof of the new building has a garden viewing area and includes a sundial unveiled in 1992. The ticket hall featured a display case advertising the Tower of London. The entrance was modified in 2016 to include a ramp in connection with new lifts to the platforms.

Monument received a makeover in the early-1990s as part of the DLR extension to Bank and the two stations are now managed as one. This was reflected in the way that common design elements were applied over both parts of the stations. The influence here was 1930s art deco, with the use of angular patterns and finishes, and carried out in conjunction with the City of London Corporation. The decade also saw the rebuild of Mansion House (1989-91), with a modern entrance provided and replacing a 1920s Holden façade. The public areas of the station were mainly clad in white rectangular tiles applied vertically and complemented by single green or yellow bands. As has become commonplace, commercial development took place overhead. Gloucester Road was also redeveloped with a shopping mall built over the surface platforms. The District and Piccadilly Line ticket halls were combined, though without affecting their external appearance.

Hammersmith was transformed as part of larger scheme with a new shopping centre and bus station, and swept away the previous Ford and Holden designs. Parts of the Harry Ford tiled external name panel were saved and reinstated in the new west end ticket hall. Preparations for the Jubilee Line led to the reconstruction of West Ham and Westminster stations by 1999. At West Ham, the formerly dilapidated LT&SR island platform 1 & 2 serving District and Hammersmith & City Line trains has been totally transformed and a new street entrance also built. Westminster was one of the flagship stations of the JLE. As well as the provision of two new Jubilee Line platforms, the District Line platforms and ticket hall were reconstructed in concrete and steel. The project was carried out in connection with the building of the Portcullis House parliamentary offices, with both undertaken by architects Michael Hopkin & Partners. The sheer size of the station, with its open escalator banks supported by metal cross-braces, makes it one of the most distinctive on the network.

The pace of change continued into the 21st Century. 2003 saw the old surface building at Fulham Broadway close with normal access now being via a modern indoor shopping centre. An additional exit was provided for use during football matches.

The work at Blackfriars was in conjunction with the Thameslink Programme and carried out between 2009 and 2012. The existing separate LU and NR surface buildings were demolished and a new joint entrance provided. This is of a curved design by Pascall & Watson architects that follows the street line and is faced with glass bearing a steel lattice frame. The platforms here have also been fully modernised, as have some of the other subsurface platforms along this stretch of the line.

Cannon Street received new entrance buildings as part of the NR station rebuild. The LU structure, opened in 2012, is a pleasing combination of concrete and glass with curving corners, reminiscent of 1930s streamlining, an impression accentuated by the provision of several silhouette exterior roundels. Victoria has gained a new entrance and ticket hall in Cardinal Place and a glass box entrance in Wilton Road.

The Jubilee Line Extension of 1999 transformed West Ham from being a rundown combination of two island platforms into a fully-accessible major transport interchange hub serving three Underground lines, the DLR and c2c main line trains. Construction is a mix of red brick, concrete and glass. To the upper left, a glazed footbridge spans Manor Road to link the high- and low-level platforms.

The rebuilding of Blackfriars stations, both Underground and National Rail, began in 2009 and was finished in time for the 2012 Olympics. Although the two operators share a single northern entrance there are separate gatelines. Underground ticket-holder passengers can also enter the station by the south bank entrance and cross the river using the main line platforms. The large blue cylinder passing through the structure is a ventilation shaft.

In 2018 work was continuing at Whitechapel to enlarge and modernise the station in readiness for the Elizabeth Line. The former four-track District Line platforms have been reduced to two, with middle platform roads 2 & 3 now a construction site. The old ticket hall, which combined both District Railway and East London Railway structures, was closed, and a temporary entrance provided at the west end of the District Line platforms. The new station was expected to be completed in 2019.

Below: Cannon Street was extensively rebuilt in 2012 in connection with the development of the National Rail station. The plain concrete and glass finishes, combined with curved elevations, produce an appearance with echoes of 1930s streamlining. The exterior roundels, complete with white 'flagpoles', are of the 'Heritage' design introduced in 2008 to mark the centenary of the roundel/bullseye.

Below right: In 2018 Victoria gained a new entrance on Wilton Road as part of the enlargement of the station and serves an extended south ticket hall. The glass and steel structure includes a lift between street and ticket hall and forms part of a wider scheme making the entire station step-free.

Above: Elements of the 1906 Harry Ford Hammersmith station façade were re-erected in the new west end ticket hall following the 1990s reconstruction of the site. Below the tiled name frieze is a new decorative work representing the reflection of Hammersmith Bridge in the River Thames.

Below: An 'Art on the Underground' display on the disused eastbound platform at Gloucester Road and framed by original 1860s DR brick-arched retaining walls. The location is regularly used for such temporary installations.